1001 Little Known Things

About Well Known People

0001.
J. Edgar Hoover, the first and most controversial Director of the FBI, once dated film actress Dorothy Lamour. It was more than just a passing fancy. Many of their friends thought the pair was destined to marry, before they drifted apart and he went on to other interests.

0002.
Barbara Bush is an avid reader, but does not watch television at all.

0003.
Actor John Wayne hated horses. He called them "filthy, disgusting creatures," and tolerated them only because western movies couldn't be made without them.

0004.
Abraham Lincoln, famous in large part for freeing men from slavery, married into a family which owned slaves.

0005.
Silent film star Charlie Chaplain, known around the world for his mime gags and funny antics, fought hard against bringing sound into the movie industry. He thought it would rob movies of their ingenuity and art, and that movies would become bland and boring.

0006.
President Harry S. Truman, the 33rd President of the United States, was a fairly proficient piano player.

0007.
John Wayne, who was born Marion Robert Morrison, was nicknamed "The Duke." It was wrongly reported that he received that nickname because of his stature and because of the masculine roles he played in his early movies. Actually, the name was derived from a dog he had in his youth.

0008.
Ronald Reagan was generally credited with declaring a "war on drugs," probably because his wife Nancy famously made it one of her favorite causes. Remember the ad campaign, "Just say NO to drugs?" Actually, it wasn't Reagan who first declared a "war on drugs." It was President Lyndon Johnson, in 1969.

0009.
Former Presidential candidate Mitt Romney lived in France as a Mormon missionary from 1966 to 1968. To this day, he speaks French fluently.

0010.
Actor and comedian Bob Hope, although British by birth, was a true American patriot. He was dedicated to the American soldier, and spent a good portion of his life going overseas to entertain the troops. The United States Congress, to recognize his efforts, named Hope the "First and only honorary veteran of the U.S. armed forces."

4

0011.
Comedian and actor Red Skelton delighted many millions of people with his portrayal of characters such as Clem Kadiddlehopper and Freddie the Freeloader. But most people did not know that Mr. Skelton was also an accomplished painter. He painted mostly clowns, perhaps a tribute to his early days working in the circus.

0012.
Texas romance novelist Dawn Brand Hawkins lived through a violent tornado when she was a small child in Lubbock, Texas. It left such an impression on her that she incorporated it into her best selling book *Trivial Pursuit*.

0013.
Stephen King, famous author, has written countless short stories and fifty two novels, including *Carrie, It, and Pet Sematery*. King is also certified to teach high school English in the state of Maine. But we suspect he's too busy finding other pursuits to follow.

0014.
We know actor Kevin Costner for his notable roles in such blockbusters as *Dances With Wolves* and *Field of Dreams*. Occasionally he made such films as *Water World,* but we can forgive him for that. What most people don't know about Costner is that he is also a successful country music singer, performing with his own band called *Kevin Costner and Modern West*.

0015.
Green bay Packer legend Bart Starr's childhood was not always a happy one. His little brother Hilton stepped on a dog bone in 1947, developed tetanus, and died three days later.

0016.
Author Dean Koontz is one of most prolific American authors of the twentieth century. He wrote under several pen names, including Brian Coffey, Leigh Nichols and David Axton. During his most prolific period, he published as many as eight novels per year. To date, his novels have sold over 470 million copies. That's two copies for every man and woman in the United States. Pretty impressive.

0017.
Muhammad Ali (born Cassius Clay) was one of the greatest boxers of all time. He was named Time Magazine's sportsman of the 20th century. Ali had a unique, outgoing personality and never lacked for self-esteem. He had his detractors as well as his supporters, but few knew the wide range of religious influence he had during his lifetime. Ali's father, also named Cassius, was born a Methodist, but he allowed his sons to be raised as Baptists. Ali later became a Methodist. In a world where most people are born and die of the same religious faith, that fact is quite remarkable.

0018.
When Green bay Packer great Bart Starr got married in college, he had to keep it a secret from his coaches at the University of Alabama. They had a bad habit of revoking scholarships for married students.

0019.
Ryan Gosling is currently an actor and director, and became a household name with *The Notebook*. It wasn't his first film, or arguably his best. But it was the film that made millions of women across the globe notice his movie star good looks and boyish charm. That boyish charm went back much farther than that, though. Back to the mid 1990s, when Ryan began his career as a member of the Mickey Mouse Club.

0020.
Edward R. Murrow was one of the most respected journalists of the twentieth century. Most Americans who lived through the middle decades of the century, when asked to name the best newscaster of their time, would likely have named either Murrow or Walter Cronkite. Both were masters at what they did, but Murrow was at his peak during the radio era. By the time television came along his career was in its twilight years. Most people don't know that Edward wasn't his real name. He changed it because he hated his given name, Egbert. We think that was a very wise decision.

0021.
Conservative talk show host Rush Limbaugh has been in radio for a long time. His first radio gig was at age sixteen. He used the pseudonym Rusty Sharp.

0022.
Barbara Bush, one of the best known and most influential Texas women in the 20th century, was actually born in Queens, New York City.

0023.
You'd think we knew everything there was to know about Mitt Romney. After all, during his run for President the Democratic Party dug up everything they thought they could use against him. The Republicans dug up everything they thought would put him in a favorable light. You'd think that all the stones would have been turned over by now, but you'd be wrong. For example, did you know that he got his name from a cousin, Milton "Mitt" Romney, who was a former quarterback for the Chicago Bears football team?

0024.
Conservative radio icon Rush Limbaugh has the most popular radio show in America, with 16.7 million listeners every weekday. Not bad for a man who was once told by a studio that he didn't have what it took to be in radio. They suggested he take a sales job instead.

0025.
John McCain III was not only a candidate for President of the United States, he was also a war hero. Much had been written about his exploits during the Vietnam War, including his being held prisoner in the infamous *Hanoi Hilton.* Apparently being a military hero is in his blood. Both his father and grandfather were four star Navy admirals.

0026.
Actor Charlton Heston, most famous for his roles in *Ben Hur* and *Planet of the Apes*, was much more than that. He was an American war hero who was a gunner on a B-25 bomber during the second world war.

0027.
President John F. Kennedy's back problems were well documented. But who knew he also had an appendectomy at age sixteen?

0028.
Whether you love O.J. Simpson or hate him, there's no denying he is once of the most recognizable of all American sports figures. His legal problems didn't begin when he was accused of the murders of Nicole Simpson and Ron Goldman, though. They went back farther than that. When Simpson was a youth, he was a member of a street gang and spent time in a youth detention facility in San Francisco.

0029.
In some of John Wayne's films, his directors purposely had him ride horses that were a bit too small for him, to make him appear even larger than life than he already was.

0030.
There's a reason why novelist John Grisham's novels tend to focus on legal issues and the law. Grisham is himself a lawyer who practiced criminal law for nine years.

0031.
Franklin Delano Roosevelt was one of the most beloved of our United States presidents. He served twelve years, longer than any other president, and was largely credited with keeping Americans' faith alive during the tragic World War II era. But he wasn't infallible. After Pearl Harbor was bombed, he ordered the imprisonment of 106,000 Japanese Americans in internment camps.

0032.
Errol Flynn, a swashbuckling, manly actor in the 1930s, was the epitome of a dashing American in his day. And in fact, he did become an American eventually. But he was actually born in Australia.

0033.
Hall of Fame quarterback Dan Marino was arguably the best quarterback the Miami Dolphins ever had. He once held the NFL record for most touchdown passes in a season. It's a shame he never went to a Super Bowl.

0034.
Jimmy Carter was known for many things. As a United States President, a peanut farmer, a staunch supporter of human rights and the Habitat for Humanity project. But not many people know that he was the very first U.S. President born in a hospital.

0035.
The "S" in President Harry S. Truman's name didn't stand for anything. Historians have been debating for decades whether to follow it with a period, which would indicate it was an initial for a longer name, or to leave out the period, which would eternally leave copy editors and readers scratching their heads. Even Truman himself seemed uncertain. Sometimes he put a period after the S, sometimes he didn't.

0036.
Jackie Onassis Kennedy spoke five languages: English, Polish, French, Spanish and Italian.

0037.

Anyone over the age of fifty remembers CBS news anchor Walter Cronkite. He was a staple in millions of living rooms during a career that spanned five decades. He was famous for his broadcast-ending catchphrase, "And that's the way it is..." and was once voted the most trusted man in America. Few people knew that during World War II he was one of a handful of journalists to fly in U.S. Army Air Corps B-17 bombers over Germany. He even got to fire a machine gun at enemy airplanes, although it's unclear whether he ever hit any of them.

0038.

Beloved actor Jimmy Stewart, as famous for his slow drawl as for his easy going manner, perhaps enchanted American audiences most in the classic *It's a Wonderful Life*. Most people not alive in that era didn't know that Stewart was also a war hero. As a pilot, he saw extensive combat over Europe and was eventually promoted to Brigadier General. Take that, Mister Potter...

0039.

Actress Betty White (*The Mary Tyler Moore Show* and *Golden Girls*) is the only woman in history who has won an Emmy for hosting a game show (*Just Men!*)

0040.

Rapper and actor Tupak Shakur had a very brief, but very successful career as a rapper and actor prior to his death in 1996. How many of you knew he also performed under the stage name *Makaveli*?

0041.

If you are a woman, and especially if you're a woman who enjoys reading, then you know who Danielle Steel is. After all, she is the best selling author living today, anywhere in the world. Her tales of affluence, romance and intrigue are eagerly awaited and purchased by the millions. But we'll bet you didn't know that Ms. Steel once married a convicted rapist and robber named Danny Zugelder, while he was still in prison. They said their vows in the prison cafeteria. Steel divorced him not long after, but it wasn't a total loss. She used the experience as a basis for one of her novels.

0042.

Janis Joplin was unorthodox in every way. She was one of the biggest names in rock music in the 1960s, yet had her roots in the blues. She was a rebel who followed her own rules. If she hadn't died at such a tender age, we no doubt would have been blessed with many more hits from this Woodstock headliner. It's actually only a coincidence, but an interesting one, that Janis went to high school with actor G.W. Bailey (*M*A*S*H, St. Elsewhere, Police Academy*) and former Dallas Cowboys head coach and sportscaster Jimmie Johnson.

0043.

Think you know everything there is to know about former U.S. President Bill Clinton? We'll bet not. Sure, maybe you knew that he was an accomplished musician. And you probably knew that he was the first president since Franklin Roosevelt to be elected twice. But we'll bet you didn't know that Clinton's life began with a tragedy. His father was killed in a tragic car accident in 1946, just three months before Bill was born.

0044.
George Takai, famous for his role as Mr. Sulu in the Star Trek series and movies, once played opposite John Wayne in a pro-Vietnam war movie called "The Green Berets."

0045.
Successful American novelist Q E Terry (*Intrigue, Intrigue 2, Twisted Clues*) was shorter than every one of her siblings. But she was still 5'10" in high school. She's been quoted as saying she hated being so tall in high school because she towered over most of the boys.

0046.
An accomplished comedian, actor and painter, Red Skelton was also very civic minded. He was a mason and a shriner. He also received an honorary degree from Emerson College in Boston, Massachusetts.

0047.
Actor Errol Flynn, by all appearances, was a dashing and successful Hollywood screen star. He did have problems, but kept them well hidden. Very few of his fans knew that he once struggled with drug addiction, and was accused of two cases of statutory rape.

0048.
What's in a name? Apparently a lot, especially if you're a Hollywood starlet. We wonder if it would have affected her career if Frances Ethel Gumm hadn't changed her name to Judy Garland.

0049.
Actor and comedian Bob Hope was a very busy man indeed. In addition to working on movies, on Broadway and in Vaudeville, he also managed to find the time to write fourteen books.

0050.
One of President Ronald Reagan's early jobs as a boy was a lifeguard. He was credited with 71 "rescues," which included pulling struggling swimmers from a pool in the tiny town of Dixon, Illinois.

0051.
Keith Richards, founding member of the *Rolling Stones*, had musical tastes other than rock and roll. His early influences included jazz greats Duke Ellington and Billie Holiday.

0052.
Former President Jimmy Carter was once part of an elite team which helped make repairs after an accident at a nuclear power plant. He was lowered into the damaged and contaminated reactor thirteen times, for short periods to minimize radiation exposure, to make the necessary repairs.

0053.
Have you ever read Richard Bachman's novels *Rage, The Long Walk, Thinner,* or *The Running Man?* Did the style seem somehow... familiar to you? Then you're probably a Stephen King fan. Richard Bachman and Stephen King are one and the same man. He used Bachman as a pseudonym, or pen name, for some of his novels.

0054.

James Galdolfini, before his untimely death, was best known for his role as Tony Soprano in *The Sopranos.* Tony was the king of a mafia empire. James came from more humble beginnings He was born to a bricklayer and a school lunch lady.

0055.

When American author Dean Koontz was a small boy, he was severely beaten on a regular basis by his alcoholic father. He attributed his very courageous mother for intervening him and saving him. He later said that the experience influenced his writing, and presumably helped him relate with the harsh realities of human nature.

0056.

Most of us who were alive in the Vietnam War years know of the story of Muhammad Ali. One of the greatest boxers in the world, he refused to go to fight a war he didn't believe in, and was thrown into prison for his refusal. But there's more to the story than that. In 1964 he failed an Army entrance exam due to low test scores. The Army didn't want him. It was only later, when the Army lowered their test standards to obtain a greater number of troops, that they decided they wanted Ali after all.

0057.

Richard M. Nixon, 37th President of the United States, was named after King Richard the Lionhearted.

0058.

CBS News anchor Walter Cronkite was a staple in Americans' living rooms for many years. His matter-of-fact style in delivering the news calmly and efficiently made him the favorite against other news anchors of his time. But long before that time, during the second world war, he was a war correspondent in a very dangerous world. One of his exploits: Landing in a war zone in a powerless glider, then witnessing and writing about the famous Battle of the Bulge.

0059.

Actor Ryan Gosling (*The Notebook*), seems to be a well adjusted and successful star on the Hollywood "A list." And, well, half the women in the world are madly in love with him, so there's that too. But Ryan wasn't always without his problems. As a child he hated going to school because he was horribly bullied and claimed he had no friends until his teen years. He was also diagnosed with ADHD around that same time. Obviously, nothing could keep this young man down, though. We think he turned out okay.

0060.

Comedian and actor Jerry Seinfeld (at last count) owns 44 Porsches.

0061.

Actor Charlton Heston was considered for the role of Sergeant J. J. Sefton in the critically acclaimed film *Stalag 17*. Heston was passed over, though, and the role was given instead to actor William Holden, who won an Oscar for his performance.

0062.

American journalist Edward R. Murrow was famous for being the calm and collected "Voice of America" during the radio era. He was largely credited with bringing down Senator Joseph McCarthy and his efforts to discredit and shame real and imagined communists in Hollywood and Washington. Murrow was a success in every way, but he came from humble beginnings. In his early years, he lived with his family in a log cabin in North Carolina. No running water, no electricity, and an out house out back. He came a long way.

0063.

Brad Pitt has had many great film roles and is one of the industry's most sought after actors. But how many of you saw him as a hitchhiker in the classic *Thelma and Louise?*

0064.

Actor Jimmy Stewart, one of the most loved movie starts of the twentieth century, charmed audiences with his slow drawl and "ah, shucks" charm. He was a versatile actor, equally comfortable in sentimental holiday classics (*It's a Wonderful Life*) and westerns (*The Man Who Shot Liberty Valence*). He was versatile in other ways as well. Who knew he was an accomplished player of the accordion?

0065.

Franklin D. Roosevelt is one of the most beloved figures in American history, and the only one of our presidents to serve four terms in office. He was a great man in his political life, but in his youth he was a bit of a rebel. Once, while vacationing with his family in Germany, young Franklin was arrested four times in one day, for various minor offenses.

0066.
20th century actor Henry Fonda was a Boy Scout who achieved the top rank of Eagle Scout, a rare feat then and now.

0067.
1960s music icon Janis Joplin (*Me and Bobby McGee, Take Another Piece of my Heart, Mercedes Benz*) was a headliner at Woodstock. *Me and Bobby McGee* was a number one hit. But she had other talents as well. Ms. Joplin was also an accomplished painter.

0068.
John McCain was and is a lot of things. A war hero during the Vietnam War. A former prisoner of war, a highly respected U.S. senator, a former U.S. Presidential candidate. The list goes on and on, but one item may surprise you. He was also a boxer. At the U.S. Naval Academy. Who knew?

0069.
Eccentric movie magnate and studio owner Howard Hughes built Houston's first radio transmitter… when he was only eleven years old.

0070.
Bill Clinton still has a lot of fans and supporters, even though he's been out of office for many years now. He still polls as one of the nation's popular former presidents, and he's famous around the world. But few people know that Clinton wasn't his surname upon birth. He gave up his surname, Blythe, and adopted his stepfather's name of Clinton.

0071.
Danielle Steel is one of America's most prolific writers. And she hasn't just written a lot of novels. She's written a lot of *great* novels. How many of you knew that she's been listed in the *Guinness Book of World Records*? She held the record for the most consecutive weeks that one of her novels was on the *New York Times Bestseller List.* For 381 consecutive weeks. That's more than seven years.

0072.
Pop sensation Selena Gomez is best known for her role in Disney Channel's *Wizards of Waverly Place.* But that wasn't her first acting gig. Remember Barney the dinosaur? Selena also appeared in *Barney and Friends* from 2002 to 2004.

0073.
Former NFL football star, actor and sportscaster O.J. Simpson is one of the most polarizing figures of the twentieth century. He's most remembered for his sensational double murder trial, in which he was acquitted. Following the murders, Simpson stayed at the home of Robert Kardashian. Father of the famous Kardashian sisters. The sisters are individually talented in their own rights, but many believe that if it weren't for their father's relationship with Simpson following the murder trial, the Kardashian sisters would have lived their lives in almost total obscurity.

0074.
Jimi Hendrix has been called one of the best instrumentalists of all time, and has been inducted into the Rock and Roll Hall of fame. Not bad for a man whose professional career as a musician spanned only four short years.

0075.

It's amazing how a man can run for President of the United States twice, be his party's official nominee once, go through several years of close scrutiny, and *still* have things that few people know about him. Republican Mitt Romney, who once lived in France in the 1960s, was involved in a fatal accident while in France. Perhaps the Democratic Party never used the story because it wasn't his fault. But a woman he worked with as a Mormon missionary was killed and Romney was seriously injured.

0076.

Harry S. Truman, the 33rd President of the United States, once moved out of the White House and across the street to the Blair House (normally the Vice President's residence and office building). The White House was in sore need of repairs and was undergoing renovation. It was during his stay at the Blair House that a dramatic assassination attempt was made on President Truman's life. Truman's would-be assassin killed a White House police officer and was sentenced to death. Truman, in a display of mercy, later commuted the man's sentence to life in prison.

0077.

We mentioned earlier in the book that novelist Richard Bachman was in fact well known writer Stephen King. King used the Bachman name to publish a few novels from 1977 to 1985. But we didn't mention where the pseudonym came from. It seems King was a big fan of the group Bachman-Turner Overdrive. And now you know…

0078.

Former Alaska Governor and vice presidential hopeful Sarah Palin can play the flute.

0079.
For a period of time in his youth, President Jimmy Carter and his wife Rosalynn, fell on hard times financially. Carter is the only U.S. President to have experienced first hand what it was like to live in government-subsidized, or "public" housing.

0080.
American boxer Muhammad Ali was as famous for his antics as he was for his boxing. He was a master at self-promotion, and recognized that boxing could be as entertaining outside the ring as within. He sometimes swore he would beat someone "or leave the country." Few people knew that he had borrowed that line from showman and professional wrester "Gorgeous George" Wagner.

0081.
President John F. Kennedy was also a Navy war hero. Everybody pretty much knows about that. But few know that he only joined the Navy because the Army didn't want him. He tried to join the Army first but they rejected him because of his bad back.

0082.
Walt Disney was many things: a successful businessman, a movie maker, a studio executive, designer and builder of incredible theme parks. But did you know he was also the original voice of Mickey Mouse?

0083.
Television star Andy Griffith (*The Andy Griffith Show, Matlock*) could play the trombone.

0084.

Albert Einstein was a German citizen who happened to be visiting the United States when Adolf Hitler came to power. He stayed in the United States and became an American citizen simply because he was afraid to return to Germany.

0085.

Many of us who were around in the 1950s and 60s remember journalist Edward R. Murrow for bringing down runaway Senator Joe McCarthy. Murrow ended McCarthy's witch hunt for supposed "communists" among American politicians and performers. But those who were around during World War II remember Murrow for something completely different. He was the first American newsman to broadcast from London during the Nazi bombing raids in 1939 and 1940. Americans sat in front of their radios spellbound by his calm reporting as bombs burst in the background.

0086.

Actor Jimmy Stewart was a lot of things. A "good ole country boy" whose modest persona became known world-wide. An Academy Award winner. A philanthroper. And, oh, yes… a real, honest-to-God war hero. The last one almost didn't happen, though. When Stewart was drafted just prior to World War II, he was told he wasn't wanted. Turned out he was too thin and didn't meet the minimum weight requirements. Most men would have been happy with that, but Stewart was a patriot as well. He hired a personal trainer to help him bulk up and gain weight… just so he could fly airplanes and get shot at by the Germans. Now *that's* patriotism.

0087.

We all know Leonard Nimoy as the unflappable Mr. Spock of *Star Trek*. But who among us remembers that he also starred in *Mission: Impossible* for two seasons?

0088.

United States Senator John McCain (R-Arizona) is famous for his heroism during the Vietnam War, when his Navy jet was shot down over Hanoi. McCain was critically injured and spent several years in the infamous *Hanoi Hilton* POW camp. But he almost didn't get to that point. Earlier in his Naval career, he was involved in a tragic accident aboard a Navy ship. In July, 1967, the USS Forrestal caught fire. McCain was critically injured while trying to help another pilot escape the flames. The tragedy claimed the lives of 134 of McCain's comrades, and was a very sad day in U.S. Naval history.

0089.

Franklin D. Roosevelt was a much-respected political leader during the turbulent World War II years. At a time when American soldiers were dying by the thousands overseas, his calm and reassuring manner soothed the nation and kept the country from breaking apart. Even those who opposed his political views regard him as a great leader. His wife, Eleanor, was equally well respected. Many considered her the stronger willed of the two. How many of you knew that Franklin and Eleanor were fifth cousins?

0090.

Conan O'Brien's father is a doctor, and his mother is a lawyer, so of course he'd follow in their footsteps and become a late night talk show host...

0091.

Actress Meryl Streep is a distant relative of William Penn, the founder of Pennsylvania.

0092.

Love him or hate him, there's no denying that O.J. Simpson was one of the greatest running backs in the history of professional football. Although he's been out of the game for a while now, he's still the only player ever to run for more that 2,000 yards in the first fourteen games of a season. Not bad for a guy who had to wear braces on his legs when he was a kid because of a bad case of rickets.

0093.

Jay Leno has played in many acting roles over the years, but the only starring role he even had in a movie was in 1989's *Collision Course*. Never heard of it? Don't feel bad. Few people have.

0094.

These days, Dan Marino is known mostly for his sports-casting skills. Not long ago, though, he was throwing passes for the Miami Dolphins, and racking up some pretty impressive records. Most football fans know that he's an NFL Hall of Famer. But most don't know that when he was in college, he was a good enough baseball player to be drafted by the Kansas City Royals. He chose to play football instead.

0095.

November 22, 1963, was one of the saddest days in American history. Most medical experts agree that President John F. Kennedy was dead when the second bullet struck him, but he was not officially pronounced dead until sometime later at Parkland Hospital. As a final tribute to her husband, Jackie Onassis Kennedy removed the wedding band from her own hand and slipped it onto her husband's pinky finger. He was buried with it.

0096.

Danielle Steel is one of the best loved American writers of all times. Her romance novels are always on best seller lists, and many have been made into successful movies. But Steel herself is a very private person. She is shy by nature and seldom makes public appearances or grants interviews. She also maintains a second home in Paris, France and spends much of her time there.

0097.

John Grisham is one of the best selling novelists of all time. He once sold two million copies on one of his book's first printings. You can't get much better than that. But if Grisham ever wants to stop writing, he can always go back into politics. That's right. He was a member of the Mississippi House of Representatives in the 1980s.

0098.

Betty White is one of the most loved comedic actresses in America. Her sharp wit and self-effacing style have made her many millions of fans. But how many knew that in her early years, lovely Miss White was also a model?

0099.
As a young girl, American novelist Dawn Brand Hawkins (*Trivial Pursuit*) attended Camp Monakiwa in West Texas. To get there she sold 164 boxes of Camp Fire Girl candy.

0100.
Iconic rapper Tupak Shakur led a troubled life from beginning to end. Much of his music was hard edged, and reflected the violence, racism and hatred he witnessed as a youth. Most people don't know, though, that both of his parents were members of the Black Panther Party.

0101.
American novelist Q E Terry (*Intrigue, Intrigue 2, Twisted Clues*) specializes in international suspense and adventure. It should be no surprise, then, that's she's quite capable of taking care of herself. When she was a young girl she was a member of the Junior National Rifle Association. Within her first year, she earned the pro-marksman badge.

0102.
Actress Judy Garland's wholesome image and girl next door charm had men all over the world falling for her. Who wouldn't want to marry lovely Dorothy from *The Wizard of Oz*? Apparently some of the Metro-Goldwyn-Mayer studio executives. Some considered Garland unattractive, and even lobbied cinematographers to shoot her from certain angles that they felt made her appear prettier.

0103.
Pop music star Bruno Mars (*Grenade, The Lazy Song*) was born Peter Gene Hernandez in 1985.

0104:
Founding member of the *Rolling Stones* Keith Richards doesn't fit the image of a choir boy, but he did indeed once fill that role. His choir was good enough to have once performed for Queen Elizabeth.

0105.
While most modern politicians come from rich and powerful families, that's not always the case. Former President Richard Nixon once said of his childhood, "We were very poor, but the glory of it was we didn't realize it."

0106.
CBS New anchor Walter Cronkite was a professional in every way. His soft spoken, no nonsense demeanor and unemotional telling of the day's events made him millions of fans across the country and the world. He was generally credited with being the first to break the news to the world that John F. Kennedy had been assassinated. And he managed to keep his composure at one of the worst events of the 1960s. But there was one time when he did break character on the air. On July 20th, 1969, when the United States had just landed men on the moon. Unable to hide his glee, he rubbed his hands together and with a very large grin uttered "Whoa, boy!" He later said he regretted the temporary lack of professionalism.

0107.
Actor Brad Pitt is a supporter of gay marriage equality. He once told a reporter, "I'll marry Angelina (Jolie) whenever everyone in America is allowed to marry their partner of choice."

0108.

Henry Fonda was one of the most beloved actors of the first half of the twentieth century. His best known works were *12 Angry Men, Mr. Roberts and The Grapes of Wrath.* When he was a mere lad of fourteen, he witnessed the lynching of a young black man who had been accused of rape.

0109.

When they were both members of the Mickey Mouse Club in Orlando, actor Ryan Gosling and singer Justin Timberlake were the best of friends. In fact, they were practically family. When Gosling's mother had to return home to Canada, Timberlake's mom became Ryan's legal guardian. He lived with the Timberlakes for six months, and they all remain quite close today.

0110.

Eccentric actor and one of the richest men in the world, Howard Hughes was a mover and shaker in Hollywood in the 1930s and 40s. In 1936, he struck and killed a pedestrian in Los Angeles. Although there was some dispute about whether he had been drinking at the time, Hughes was eventually cleared of all charges.

0111.

Walt Disney's first cartoons weren't of mice and funny dogs with big floppy ears. No, his early cartoons began in high school, when he drew them for the school newspaper. The themes were serious and patriotic and generally in support of World War I, which was still going on at the time.

0112.
William Shatner hates seeing himself on screen and has never watched a single episode of the *Star Trek* television show.

0113.
When guitar hero and Woodstock legend Jimi Hendrix was a young boy, he often hid in a closet for long periods of time. It was his only means of escape from an abusive family life.

0114.
Politician and news commentator Sarah Palin can also add former athlete to her resume. In high school she was on a girls basketball team that won the 1982 Alaska State Championship.

0115.
Oh, and Sarah's nickname on that team, because of her spirit and competitive attitude, was "Sarah Barracuda."

0116.
Legendary physicist Albert Einstein was most well known for his theories of relativity and the time and space continuum. Most people don't know that the Manhattan Project, which was the development of the atomic bomb by American scientists, owed its existence to Einstein. It was Einstein who predicted that German scientists would be working to develop the atomic bomb, and who urged President Roosevelt to do likewise.

0117.
Some of you may have suspected as such, but now you'll know for sure. Raven-haired pop music princess Selena Gomez was indeed named after Tejano music star Selena.

0118.
20th century actor and television star Andy Griffith was once a high school teacher. Seriously. He once taught drama and music at Goldsboro High School in Goldsboro, North Carolina.

0119.
Jay Leno. Actor, comedian, night show host, wrestler… Wait a minute. How did wrestler get in there? In 1998, Leno completed a match for the World Confederation of Wrestling. It was a pay-per-view event, and many people missed it. We did.

0120.
Actor Leonard Nimoy (*Star Trek, Mission: Impossible*) used to be Sergeant Nimoy, when he served in the United States Army in the 1950s. He served with fellow actor Ken Berry (*Mayberry, R.F.D., Mama's Family*)

0121.
Recording star Bruno Mars (*Grenade, The Lazy Song*) performed in his family's band at the tender age of four. He wowed audiences with his spot-on impersonation of Elvis Presley.

0122.
Actress Meryl Streep, although German in heritage, speaks fluent Italian.

0123.
Conan O'Brien is most famous for hosting the late night talk show with the same name. But those of you who were fans of *The Simpsons* may have vague memories of seeing his name in credits even before his late night gig. Conan was a writer and producer for *The Simpsons* from 1991 to 1993.

0124.
Captain James T. Kirk, of *Star Trek* fame, will be an Aries, born March 22, 2233.

0125.
Actor and director William Shatner (*Star Trek, T.J. Hooker*) suffers from Tinnitus, a constant ringing in the ears. He reportedly developed the condition as the result of an accident on the *Star Trek* (series) set in 1967.

0126.
Late night talk show host David Letterman collected model racing cars when he was a boy. That shouldn't be a surprise, since he grew up in the shadows of the Indianapolis Motor Speedway.

0127.
Country music sweetheart Taylor Swift went to Nashville to make it big at the tender age of fourteen.

0128.
American actor Sam Elliot is one of the most recognizable faces in Hollywood. He's well suited for tough guy roles, like motorcyclists and cowboys. But his breakthrough role came as a big hearted softy in *Mask*, when he co-starred with Cher.

0129.
Radio talk show host Rush Limbaugh is highly successful, boasting the most popular radio show in the country. But few people know that he used to be almost completely deaf. His career could well have ended then, but with the help of cochlear implants, he was able to go on.

0130.
Captain James T. Kirk, from the *Star Trek* series and movies, is indeed a fictional character. But he is as famous as Snooki, so we're including him in this book, okay? Anyway, before Captain Kirk commanded the *U.S.S. Enterprise,* Lieutenant Kirk commanded the *U.S.S. Farragut.*

0131.
Comedian and talk show host Jimmy Kimmel (*Jimmy Kimmel Live*) was raised a Roman Catholic and was once an alter boy.

0132.
Roy Rogers was a legendary cowboy, a movie star in the 1930s and 40s, and a hero to millions of young boys around the world. Many of you know he built a museum to showcase his career in the city of Victorville, California. But how many of you knew that he and wife Dale Evans lived nearby, and went to the museum almost daily to shake hands, sign autographs, and talk to their fans?

0133.
Cher is short for Cherilyn Sarkisian. Cher is much easier to spell…

0134.
If someone comes up to you and asks if you know someone named Martina Mariea Schiff, you'll probably give them a weird look, assume they're asking for money and walk away very quickly in the other direction. That is, unless you're a big time country music fan. Then you'll likely hang around and carry on a conversation. Because you'll know that Martina Mariea Schiff is none other than country recording legend Martina McBride.

0135.
Buddy Holly, who hailed from Lubbock, Texas, is still credited with being one of the most influential founders of rock and roll. His hits *Peggy Sue* and *That'll be the Day* are still played on mainstream radio more than fifty years after his death. Not bad, considering his career was less than two years in duration.

0136.
Singer John Denver (*Country Roads, Rocky Mountain High*) was like a lot of other singers when he changed his given name to one easier for the public to relate to. His birth name was Henry John Deutschendorf, Jr.

0137.
Country music legend Johnny Cash always opened his concerts with the classic *Folsom Prison Blues.*

0138.
In 1969, John Lennon legally modified his name to include "Ono" as a tribute to his wife Yoko Ono. His name after that date was officially John Winston Ono Lennon.

0139.
Mac Davis is just one of many outstanding singers and songwriters to come out of Lubbock, Texas. He's also an actor, appearing in *North Dallas Forty* with Nick Nolte. Did you know he wrote many of Elvis Presley's most cherished hits, including *In the Ghetto* and *Memories*?

0140.
Country music star Sara Evans was hit by a car when she was eight years old. She was confined to a wheelchair for almost a year, and there were fears she'd never walk again.

0141.
Actor Gary Cooper (*High Noon, Pride of the Yankees*) had much better success in his acting career than in his earlier endeavors. As an actor he was one of the most beloved actors in Hollywood and won more awards than he could count. But in his younger years he failed miserably as an electric sign salesman.

0142.
Most of us remember Ringo Starr, from *The Beatles*. But how many of you knew that *Starr* was originally *Starkey*?

0143.
Blonde beauty and singer Jessica Simpson once auditioned for *The Mickey Mouse Club* but wasn't selected. She later said she was intimidated by the other performers' talents and froze up when it was her turn on the stage.

0144.
You can call her Madonna, or you can call her by her birth name: Madonna Louise Ciccone. Or, you can even call her Veronica. That's another name she adopted as a confirmation name in 1966.

0145.
Marilyn Monroe spent most of her childhood in foster homes. She never met her father, and only saw a photograph of him one time. She remembered him as looking somewhat like Clark Gable.

0146.
Paul McCartney (*The Beatles, Paul McCartney and Wings*) is officially listed in the *Guinness book of World Records* as "The most successful composer and songwriter of all time."

0147.
Actress Jennifer Anniston's ancestry is a complicated one. She is at least part Greek, Italian, Scottish and Irish.

0148.
Actor Clint Eastwood (*Dirty Harry, Kelly's Heroes*) was in the Army during the Korean War. His job? Lifeguard, of all things.

0149.
Actress Meryl Streep has some pretty good pipes. Her rendition of *Mama Mia* peaked at Number 8 on Portuguese music charts in 2008.

0150.
As a young boy, Al Pacino (*The Godfather, Scarface, Scent of a Woman*) had several nicknames. Oddly enough, or maybe a premonition of things to come, one of his nicknames was "The Actor."

0151.
Beautiful actress Kristen Stewart (Bella Swan in the *Twilight* saga) only went to school through the seventh grade. He finished her studies and got her high school diploma through correspondence courses.

0152.
If actor Leonard Nimoy, of *Star Trek* fame, ever invites you over for dinner, ask him if you can see his ears. When the original *Star Trek* series was cancelled, he kept the last pair of Mr. Spock's pointed ears as a souvenir.

0153.

In a truly bizarre case of celebrity stalking, talk show host Conan O'Brien was allegedly stalked by a priest named Father David Ajemian. This has gone on since 2006 and has taken several turns, including a restraining order and the church taking away Ajemian's right to act as a priest.

0154.

William Shatner, because of his role as Captain Kirk in *Star Trek*, is considered the quintessential American hero. Perhaps that's because most people consider the origin of the *U.S.S. Enterprise* captain to be the United States. But here's a shocker. Shatner's actually Canadian.

0155.

Actor Kevin Bacon (*National Lampoon's Animal House, Footloose*) may be laid back, but he's no slouch. He attended the Pennsylvania Governor's School for the Arts, under a full scholarship.

0156.

Country music mega star Shania Twain was born in Canada. Her birth name was Eilleen Regina Edwards.

0157.

Captain Kirk, of *Star Trek* fame, hails from Riverside, Iowa. The city even has a monument to prove it. It says "Future Birthplace of Captain James T. Kirk." Really.

0158.
Late night talk show host David Letterman went to high school at Broad Ripple High in Indianapolis… with Marilyn Tucker, the future wife of Dan Quayle. Maybe if David had married Marilyn instead of Quayle, he'd have been Vice President.

0159.
In 2011, Late Night host David Letterman received a real death threat from a group with ties to Al-Qaeda. The government was sufficiently concerned to investigate the case. Letterman, ever the jokester, claimed Jay Leno was behind it.

0160.
Country music singer Taylor Swift is famously known for writing songs about ex boyfriends. But it goes both ways. Joe Jonas and John Meyer have both written songs about her.

0161.
Actress Ashley Greene, who played Alice Cullen in the *Twilight* movies, chose acting as a second career She first tried being a runway model, but at 5'4" she was considered by most designers to be too short.

0162.
Actor and director Nicolas Cage (*Con-Air, Raising Arizona*), is an avid collector of comic books, and even created one of his own, called *Voodoo Child.*

0163.

Actor Ben Affleck (*Pearl Harbor*) is an avid and very talented poker player.

0164.

Singer, actress and comedienne Cher is many things to many people. Along with everything else, her striking beauty has been noticed as well. World famous *Madame Tussauds Wax Museum* created a life-size wax statue of Cher and named her one of the five most beautiful women in history.

0165.

1930s and 40s movie cowboy icon Roy Rogers actually has three stars on the Hollywood Walk of fame. One for his acting, one for his success in radio, and one for his music.

0166.

Country music singer Martina McBride has a voice so big, she must be a giant, right? Wrong. Despite her commanding presence and powerful voice, she's a tiny girl at 5'2".

0167.

Actor Hugh Jackman (*The X-Men*) once aspired to be an "airplane chef." He explained that as a young man he was so impressed with airline food that he assumed there was a chef in the back of the plane making it. Apparently he didn't fly the same airline we do.

0168.
Singer and actress Rihanna's birth name is Robyn. Robyn Rihanna Fenty. Maybe that's why she sings like a bird.

0169.
Buddy Holly is one of the most famous, and still popular, of the early rock and roll pioneers. But did you know he only produced three albums during his short career, before he was killed in a plane crash in 1959?

0170.
Singer John Denver (*Annie's Song*) was normally a pretty mellow guy. But not always. After he divorced his first wife, Annie Martell, he was so enraged by the property settlement that he used a chainsaw to cut their bed in half.

0171.
Many people believed that country music star Johnny Cash was an ex convict with a surly disposition and a mean streak. However, those who knew him best knew him as anything but. They said he was a kind and loving man. As for the prison thing… it's probably because he empathized with convicts and performed free shows inside of prisons. In reality, he was arrested a few times for misdemeanors, in which he was either fined or spent a night in jail. But he never went to prison except to perform.

0172.
In early 1977, a pretty little girl named Shakira Isabel Mebarek Ripoll was born in Columbia. That's quite a name. No wonder she shortened it to Shakira.

0173.

Bart Starr, the legendary quarterback for the Green bay Packers, is best known for the records he broke, the five Super Bowls he won, and for having the highest quarterback rating in NFL history. But one thing he isn't known for was being greedy. His first signing bonus for the Packers was a paltry $6500.

0174.

Did you know that people close to Osama bin Laden once tried to assassinate President Bill Clinton? It happened in the Philippines in 1996. The plan was to plant a bomb on a bridge that Clinton's car was scheduled to drive over. The plot was discovered and plans were changed mere hours before it was to take place.

0175.

Actor Tommy Lee Jones *(Lonesome Dove, Men in Black)* has played in a lot of memorable roles over the years. But few people remember his first film role, as a bit player in the classic movie *Love Story.*

0176.

Jackie Kennedy Onassis moved away from the United States out of fear for the lives of her children. Her husband, President John F. Kennedy, was assassinated in 1963. Her brother in law, Bobby Kennedy, was assassinated in 1968. The former first lady remarked to a friend, "If they are to continue killing Kennedys, my children are targets. I want to leave this country."

0177.
Former Miami Dolphin quarterback and Hall of Famer Dan Marino has been successful at many different things. In fact, you could technically call him "Dr. Marino." he was awarded an honorary doctorate degree in journalism from the University of Pittsburgh.

0178.
John Lennon of *The Beatles* wasn't just an accomplished songwriter and musician. He was also a very talented poet and artist.

0179.
American author Dean Koontz is best known for his "can't-put-down" classics such as the *Odd Thomas* series and his *Frankenstein* series. He once wrote the screenplay for an episode of the *CHiPs* TV series. Yes. The one with Eric Estrada and Larry Wilcox as California Highway Patrol motorcycle cops. The episode was titled "Counterfeit."

0180.
When romance writer Dawn Brand Hawkins (*Trivial Pursuit*) was eight years old, her pet parakeet got away. Hawkins was frantic, until she heard that her grandmother, while visiting a friend a quarter mile away, was somehow tracked down and attacked by the bird. Hawkins managed to keep the bird anyway, and he was her constant companion until age sixteen.

0181.
Ringo Starr, drummer for *The Beatles*, exudes rock and roll.
But when asked who his musical influences were as a youth,
his answer surprised many. Starr, an Englishman, listed
American country music singers gene Autry, Hank Williams,
Hank Snow and Buck Owens.

0182.
Actress Betty White has endeared herself to tens of millions
of Americans, and many other millions around the world.
Her down-home style plays well for audiences, and she's
won many awards for her work. For many people, her
greatest performances were as Rose in the comedy series *The
Golden Girls.* But how many of you knew she was first
offered the role of unabashed man-chaser Blanch?

0183.
Ever heard of a man named Lesane Parish Crooks? Probably
not, huh? But if you saw a photograph of Tupak Shakir, the
rapper and actor who was shot down and murdered in Las
Vegas in 1971, you'd recognize him. Tupak Shakur and
Lesane Parish Crooks were one and the same.

0184.
Actor Henry Fonda was offered an opportunity to serve his
country during World War II by making patriotic movies in
Hollywood. Instead, he chose not to. He signed on with the
Navy as an enlisted supply troop. He said he didn't "want to
be in some fake war in a Hollywood studio."

0185.
Keith Richards, of the mega band *The Rolling Stones,* has always freely admitted using drugs over the course of his career. Despite his honesty, he says he's been clean for over twenty years now, and many people refuse to believe him.

0186.
Former United States President Richard Nixon was an athlete, of sorts, in high school. He played football, but rode the bench most of the time. Turns out he was much better in scholastics and in debate class.

0187.
By the time she was four years old, singer and songwriter Carol King was an accomplished piano player.

0188.
Famous director and film maker Howard Hughes had a love for flying airplanes. Many of you knew about the "Spruce Goose," an airplane he developed for use in World War II. The plane was made almost entirely of plywood, since steel was in short supply. At the time it was the largest airplane in the world, but the war ended without it being needed. But you knew all that. Did you know that Hughes' flying abilities helped him set several world flying records?

0189.
Playboy publisher Hugh Hefner was so smitten with Marilyn Monroe after she posed in his magazine that he purchased the crypt next to hers at Westwood Village Memorial Park Cemetery. So that he could be close to her after their deaths.

0190.
Singer Beyonce Knowles, more commonly known simply as Beyonce, is of African, Creole, French and Native American Ancestry.

0191.
Singer and sometimes actress Madonna follows the Kabbalah faith. That's why she never does concerts on Fridays.

0192.
Pop music sensation Selena Gomez is highly successful today, combining an acting career with a successful music career. But she came from humble roots. She was born to a sixteen year old single mother, and they struggled financially through most of her childhood.

0193.
Actor Brad Pitt (*Ocean's Eleven, Fight Club*) has had so many great roles in popular movies. But that's not where he originally set his sights. He graduated from college with a degree in journalism.

0194.
Jimi Hendrix's performance playing *The Star Spangled Banner* on an electric guitar was one of the most memorable performances at 1969's Woodstock festival. His appearance, with typical "hippie" clothing of the day and an oversize unkempt afro haircut, led many to assume he was another anti-war peace loving activist. Actually, just a few years before, Hendrix was a soldier in the U.S. Army and a trained paratrooper.

0195.

One of the most beloved novelists of the twentieth century is John Grisham, whose police and courtroom dramas keep millions of faithful readers captivated. But he wasn't always such a great success. When he was younger, one of his jobs was selling men's underwear at a department store.

0196.

Actress Judy Garland was most known for her breakout role as Dorothy Gale in *The Wizard of Oz*. But in reality, she performed in dozens of roles over her short life. She almost didn't get the *Wizard of Oz* role. She wasn't the studio's first choice. They wanted Shirley Temple, but couldn't make a deal with *20th Century Fox,* Miss Temple's studio at the time.

0197.

Former Governor of Alaska Sarah Palin was once a beauty queen. She won the Miss Wasilla (Alaska) pageant in 1984. She was second runner up in the Miss Alaska pageant that same year.

0198.

Legendary physicist Albert Einstein has no grave. When he died in 1955 at the age of 76, his brain was removed so that it could be examined. It was thought that by examining his brain under a microscope, scientists might be able to determine why Einstein was so much more intelligent that most other humans. As for the rest of his remains? They were cremated and scattered in an undisclosed location.

0199.

Walt Disney dropped out of school at age sixteen to join the Army during World War I. The Army rejected him for being too young. Imagine how different the world would be if he had made the Army his career instead of cartooning.

0200.

Since the Army wouldn't take him, Disney joined the Red Cross instead. For a year he was assigned to France, where he drove an ambulance.

0201.

Beloved actor and director Andy Griffith (*The Andy Griffith Show, Matlock*), once played in a movie called *No Time for Sergeants*. Don Knotts was also in the movie, and was the beginning of a long collaboration between the pair. *No Time for Sergeants* was also the inspiration for the *Gomer Pyle, U.S.M.C.* television show.

0202.

Novelist Darrell Maloney (*The Secession of Texas, Final Dawn, Countdown to the Apocalypse*) has a recurring character in many of his novels named Sarah Anna Spear. It's not just a coincidence. Sarah Anna Spear was an old girlfriend who died in a tragic accident. He never quite got over her, so he keeps her alive in his novels.

0203.

Jay Leno, of *The Tonight Show with Jay Leno*, was one of the witnesses called to testify at Michael Jackson's child molestation trial.

0204.

Actress Meryl Streep is considered a classic beauty. But not by everybody. She was turned down for the leading female role in Dino De Laurentis' remake of *King Kong*. He reportedly remarked to his casting director, "She's ugly. Why did you bring her to me?"

0205.

Actor Leonard Nimoy played Mr. Spock in the original *Star Trek* television series as well as several *Star Trek* movies. He invented the famous split-fingered "Vulcan salute" himself. He said it reminded him of the way Jewish priests held their hands when giving blessings.

0206.

Late night talk show host Conan O'Brien provided the voice of talk show host Dave Endocrine in 2013's *Batman Returns.*

0207.

Actor, director, and *Priceline* representative William Shatner can be called one of the most recognizable and successful figures in Hollywood. But that wasn't always the case. There was a time in his early career when he struggled financially, and lived in a camper shell on the back of his pickup truck. The camper, he said, could be set up on its own legs and resembled a spaceship. Irony at its best.

0208.

Comedian and talk show host Jimmy Kimmel (*Jimmy Kimmel Live*) knows how to play the bass clarinet.

0209.
Country music star Taylor Swift is the youngest person to have a song she wrote and performed make it to the number one spot on the country music chart. (*Our Song*, 2008)

0210.
Country music star Martina McBride is very family oriented. She has two brothers and a sister. The brothers, Martin and Steve, play in her band during her concerts.

0211.
Author Q E Terry (*Intrigue, Intrigue 2, Twisted Clues*), is Native American and English by birth. She has attended spiritual retreats in sweat lodges many times, and says she misses going every time there's a full moon.

0212.
Captain James T. Kirk, of *Star Trek* fame, is fictional, but much of his background has been documented in various episodes and movies. For example, did you know that when he was given command of the *U.S.S. Enterprise,* he was the youngest captain in Starfleet Command?

0213.
Cher is famous for many things. Singer, actress, comedian, fashion trendsetter. And she's been doing all those things very well for awhile now. Cher is the only recording artist to have a number one song on the *Billboard* chart in each of six consecutive decades.

0214.
1940s cowboy movie star Roy Rogers struggled early in his career. Sometimes instead of accepting money for gigs, he accepted other things instead. He once sang a song on the radio in exchange for a lemon pie. He later married the woman who presented him with the pie. She was Rogers' first wife, Arline.

0215.
Rock and roll legend Buddy Holly's last name was actually "Holley." It was misspelled on a contact early in his career, and he kept the misspelled version as his professional name.

0216.
After President John F. Kennedy's famous speech in West Berlin, in which he uttered the words *Ich bin ein Berliner* ("I am a Berliner") he was cheered by a crowd of more than a million people. He was overhead remarking to a close friend, "Enjoy this day. We will not have another day this good, as long as we live."

0217.
David Letterman has been a successful late night talk show host for over thirty years, and we have a tendency to think he's always performed in that role. But his first gig in television was as a weatherman on WNTS Radio in Indianapolis.

0218.
Drummer Ringo Starr (*The Beatles*) contracted peritonitis at age six, and was in a coma for three days.

0219.

When John Lennon of *The Beatles* was a mere lad of five, his parents divorced. His father forced young John to decide which parent he wanted to live with. Initially John chose his father, but then had a change of heart and went with his mother. His father did not contact him again for twenty years.

0220.

Infamous outlaw William H. Bonney, better known as *Billy the Kid*, had at least two other known aliases: William Henry McCarty, Jr. and Henry Antrim.

0221.

Country music legend Johnny Cash was named "J. R. Cash" because his parents couldn't decide on a name. He himself chose "John" later and changed it to his legal name.

0222.

When country music singer Sara Evans divorced Craig Schelske in 2007, she got the kids, and he got the alimony. Evans was ordered to pay him half a million dollars over a ten year period.

0223.

Beloved actor Gary Cooper (*High Noon, Pride of the Yankees*) carefully cultivated a squeaky clean persona, but there were indeed a few skeletons in his closet. Although he was married in 1950, he had an affair with actress Patricia Neal, who became pregnant. Cooper paid for an abortion to avoid a scandal.

0224.
Singer John Denver (*Rocky Mountain High, Annie*) decided he didn't like high school in Ft. Worth, Texas. So he borrowed his father's car, drove to California to hang out with friends, and never went back.

0225.
Blonde bombshell singer Jessica Simpson and husband Nick Lachey once appeared on an *MTV* show called *Newlyweds: Nick and Jessica*. Many of you knew that. But how many of you knew that the show was originally written for Michael Jackson and Lisa Marie Presley?

0226.
Singer and actress Madonna has always been a rebel when it came to her music, pushing the envelope with her costumes and her behavior. But she was that way long before she became a successful musician. In middle school, she was known to sometimes lift her skirt so the boys in her class could see her underwear.

0227.
Marilyn Monroe despised actor Tony Curtis after she heard that he described kissing her, "like kissing Hitler."

0228.
When President Harry S. Truman left office, he survived for a time on his monthly army pension of $113 per month. At that time, there was no pension package for either former Presidents or former Senators.

0229.
Paul McCartney's song *Yesterday* is pretty popular. It's been covered by over 2,200 other artists, according to the *Guinness Book of World Records.*

0230.
Actress Jennifer Aniston's godfather was actor Telly Savalas *(Kojak, Kelly's Heroes).*

0231.
When actor Clint Eastwood (*Dirty Harry, Kelly's Heroes*) was in the Army, he survived a plane crash. He was on board a bomber that crashed into the Pacific Ocean near Point Reyes, California. He swam three miles to shore.

0232.
Acting legend Andy Griffith shied away from politics. He once said it was better for people to think of him as not very bright, instead of going to Congress and confirming their suspicions. That's why he declined an offer from the Democratic National Committee to run against North Carolina Senator Jesse Helms in 1989.

0233.
Jay Leno, host of *The Tonight Show with Jay Leno,* is a renowned actor and comedian. He'd also a major car guy. Most fans know about his extensive collection of automobiles and motorcycles. But did you also know he writes a regular column for *Popular Mechanics* magazine?

0234.

Actor Al Pacino (*The Godfather, Scent of a Woman, Scarface*), has been a leading ladies man and has had relationships with several Hollywood beauties. He also has three children. But he has never married.

0235.

Successful and stunning Hollywood actress Kristen Stewart (the *Twilight* saga) seemingly has it all. But she also has an unfulfilled dream. She wants to go to college and study literature. Then she wants to become a writer.

0236.

Kevin Bacon (*Footloose, Animal House, A Few Good Men*) isn't just an actor with a tasty surname. He's also a musician who has released six albums with his band called *The Bacon Brothers.*

0237.

Singer and songwriter Shania Twain can boast that her album *Come on Over* is the best selling album of all time, by any female act in any genre, and is the best selling country music album ever.

0238.

Actor, producer and director Denzel Washington almost chose his college based solely on the football team's name. When he was in high school, his team was called the Red Raiders. He wanted to attend college at Texas Tech University in Lubbock, Texas, simply because their football team had the same name. He wound up going to Fordham instead.

0239.

Actor and director Nicolas Cage named his second son Kal-El, after *Superman's* birth name.

0240.

Actor George Clooney was born to be a star. He was the son of a beauty queen and a host of *American Movie Classics*. How could he possibly go wrong?

0241.

Actor Clint Eastwood (*Dirty Harry, The God, the Bad, and the Ugly*) weighed over eleven pounds when he was born. Nurses at the hospital nicknamed him "Samson."

0242.

Singer and actress Rihanna has a variety of tattoos. One that puzzles many of her fans is the one written in Arabic on her ribcage. Translated, it means, "Freedom in Messiah."

0243.

Colombian singer, dancer and model Shakira was born on ground hog day. We don't know whether or not she saw her shadow.

0244.

When Erich Segal wrote the classic screenplay for *Love Story*, he based the main character of Oliver (played by Ryan O'Neal in the film) on two men he knew in college: Tommy Lee Jones and Al Gore.

0245.
Singer and songwriter Carol King dropped out of the spotlight for several years, but popped up again in several episodes of *Gilmore Girls*. She played Sophie, who fittingly enough owned the Stars Hollow music store.

0246.
Singer Beyonce Knowles, more commonly known simply as Beyonce, is a direct descendent of Acadian leader Joseph Broussard.

0247.
Actor Brad Pitt (*Ocean's Eleven, Fight Club*) has had many memorable movie roles over the years. But who can remember the bit parts he played in the television shows *Growing Pains* and *Dallas*?

0248.
Paul McCartney's response when learning of John Lennon's murder in December, 1980 was short and sweet. He merely said, "It's a drag."

0249.
Singer Michael Jackson was the first American to appear on a commercial in the Union of Soviet Socialist Republics, in 1989.

0250.
Singer and *American Idol* winner Carrie Underwood gave up on singing when she graduated from high school. Instead, she went to work at a zoo, and then a veterinary clinic.

0251.
Actor Bob Crane was most famous for playing Colonel Robert Hogan on *Hogan's Heroes*. But he also played the drums, good enough to play for the Connecticut Symphony and the Norwalk Symphony orchestras.

0252.
Hollywood beauty Jessica Alba (*Dark Angel, Fantastic Four*) had a rough time as a kid. She had pneumonia several times, partially collapsed lungs and a ruptured appendix.

0253.
Pop star singer, songwriter and actress Christina Aguilera had a very abusive childhood. She has said that music was her escape, a way of insulating herself from the abuse.

0254.
Phil Robertson (*Duck Dynasty*) once played quarterback on the Louisiana Tech University football team. He was the number one quarterback on the team. The number two, right behind him, was Hall of Famer Terry Bradshaw.

0255.
Speaking of Terry Bradshaw, he suffers from short term memory loss, which he attributes to his NFL playing days.

0256.
Actress and model Emma Watson (*Harry Potter, The Bling Thing*) is famously British. But she was actually born in Paris, and speaks French.

0257.
Actor, producer and rapper Will Smith is a Christian by faith, but he calls himself "a student of all religions."

0258.
Actor Audie Murphy (*To Hell and Back, Whispering Smith*) was one of the most decorated military veterans in history, including the award of the Congressional Medal of Honor for heroism during World War II

0259.
Singer Marilyn Manson was born Brian Hugh Warner. He got his stage name by mixing the names of Marilyn Monroe and Charles Manson.

0260.
Legendary Dallas Cowboys football coach Tom Landry graduated from the University of Texas with a degree in industrial engineering. The only engineering he ever did, though, was engineering two Super Bowl victories and five NFC titles for the Cowboys. But that still counts.

0261.
Actress and pop music star Selena Gomez is seemingly the poster girl for self confidence and positive self-esteem. But it wasn't always that way. Selena has said that as a school girl she was bullied, was very unpopular, and had no self confidence at all.

0262.
Actor Christopher Plummer (*The Sound of Music, The Man Who Would be King*) speaks French fluently.

0263.
Legendary musician Bruce Springsteen never went to Vietnam. He failed his induction physical because of a concussion he suffered in an earlier motorcycle accident.

0264.
Medal of Honor recipient Audie Murphy starred in over 40 feature films, including his own biopic *To Hell and Back*. But his only television series was *Whispering Smith*.

0265.
Singing legend Bob Dylan recorded several songs for Columbia Records under the pseudonym Blind Boy Grunt.

0266.
Legendary Baltimore Colts quarterback Johnny Unitas was an extra in the movie *Runaway Bride* (1999). He can be seen sitting on a bench outside a bakery.

0267.
Actor Nick Nolte has had many memorable roles over the years (*The Prince of Tides, Cape Fear, The Deep, 48 Hrs.*) Perhaps it was destiny that he be considered among Hollywood royalty. After all, his middle name is King.

0268.
General Douglas Macarthur, besides being a five star general in the United States Army, was the only American to become a field marshal in the Philippine Army.

0269.
Charley Pride made it big in country music, and is one of the few African Americans who has chosen the genre. But country music isn't his only talent. He was a good enough baseball player in his younger days to pitch for one of the New York Yankees' minor league teams.

0270.
Singer Lady Gaga got her stage name from a song by the band Queen called *Radio Ga Ga.*

0271.
Rapper and actor Eminem spent three years in ninth grade, then dropped out of school at the age of seventeen.

0272.
Actor and comedian Billy Crystal (*When Harry Met Sally, City Slickers, Soap*) attended Marshall University (West Virginia) on a baseball scholarship.

0273.
Actress and producer Julia Roberts (*Pretty Woman, Steel Magnolias, Erin Brockovich*) comes from a family of actors. Eric Roberts, Lisa Roberts Gillian, and Emma Roberts are all relatives.

0274.
Novelist Darrell Maloney (*A Secret Life, The Secession of Texas, The Cleansing*) has a way of cheating death. He once witnessed an airplane crash that killed 70 people less than fifty yards away from him. When he was in the U.S. Air Force during Operation Desert Storm, he lived in a housing area called Khobar Towers. The building he lived in was torn apart by a terrorist truck bomb several years later, and his old room collapsed five stories into the courtyard below.

0275.
Taylor Swift's middle name is Alison. With only one l.

0276.
George Clooney's clean cut image goes back a very long way. As a youth in Mason, Ohio he was an alter boy.

0277.
Actor and producer Leonardo DiCaprio (*The Aviator, What's eating Gilbert Grape, Titanic*) speaks German fluently.

0278.

Actress Kate Winslet (*The Titanic, Sense and Sensibility*) has been appointed a *Commander of the Order of the British Empire.* It's a big deal if you're British.

0279.

Martina McBride isn't just a country music legend. She's a woman of faith and family values, and gives back to her community. She's also very much into charity work. She has hosted the Middle Tennessee YWCA charity auction for nineteen straight years and has helped them raise more than $600,000.

0280.

Actor Josh Brolin has made some really memorable movies lately (*No Country for Old Men, American Gangster, True Grit, Men in Black 3*). But who remembers way back in 1985, when he was just one of those kids in *The Goonies*?

0281.

Cher has always been ultra-talented. When she was only eleven years old, she produced the play *Oklahoma*, much to the delight of her teachers and classmates. When most of us were eleven, we couldn't even spell "Oklahoma."

0282.

On December 8th, 1980, Mark David Chapman shot John Lennon of *The Beatles* four times in New York City. But that wasn't the first encounter the two men had. Chapman had approached Lennon earlier that day, and Lennon autographed a copy of the album *Double Fantasy* for him.

0283.

One of rock and roll legend Buddy Holly's blockbuster hits was *That'll be the Day*. We've all heard it a million times on the radio, and many albums of greatest rock and roll hits has included it. But did you know the song was inspired by John Wayne? In the movie *The Searchers*, Wayne uttered the phrase several times, and it meant, in effect, "ain't happening."

0284.

Actress Ashley Judd (*Double Jeopardy, Norma Jean and Marilyn, Kiss the Girls*) moved around a lot as a child. By the time she graduated from high school, she attended thirteen schools.

0285.

Singer John Denver (*Rocky Mountain High*) was an accomplished songwriter as well. One of his early songs was called *Babe, I Hate to Go*. It was destined to be a hit. What, you never heard of it? Maybe that's because it was renamed *Leaving on a Jet Plane* before Peter, Paul and Mary released it and it went to number one.

0286.

Most of us have seen Roy Rogers as a cowboy in old black and white movies. He could ride, he could shoot, he could play a guitar and croon pretty songs to whichever actress was playing opposite him in the movie. But not a lot of people these days know that Rogers also had a very successful singing career outside the movies. He formed a very successful band, the *Sons of the Pioneers*, who put out such classics as *Tumbling Tumbleweeds* and *Cool Water*.

0287.
William Bonney, better known as Billy the Kid, is one of the most famous outlaws from the American West. But most historians now agree that even though birth records were inconclusive, he was actually born in New York City.

0288.
Country music singer Johnny Cash came off as a rough, tough, no-nonsense man who was always just one step ahead of the law. In reality, he spent time in the United States Air Force as a young man, and was assigned to a Security Service (Police) Squadron.

0289.
Actor Gary Cooper (*High Noon, Pride of the Yankees*) was buried twice. He was originally buried in Culver City, California shortly after his death in 1961. Later, his widow moved to New York and took him with her. He was reburied in Southampton, New York in 1974.

0290.
Drummer Ringo Starr (*The Beatles*) had a lot of health issues as a boy and young man. Besides having appendicitis and then peritonitis, he later contracted tuberculosis. For the latter, he was confined to a sanatorium for two years.

0291.
Actor William Devane (*Knott's Landing, Red Flag, The Missiles of October*) is the son of Franklin D. Roosevelt's chauffeur.

0292.
In the early 1950s, Elvis Presley worked as a truck driver for the Crown Electric Company. After auditioning for a local band, he was told, "Stick to truck driving. You'll never make it as a singer."

0293.
Singer and actress Madonna was a cheerleader in high school. Really. She was also a straight-A student.

0294.
Rob Mariano, winner of *Survivor: Philippines*, was a Christmas baby, born December 25, 1975.

0295.
Actress Farrah Fawcett (*Charlie's Angels, The Burning Bed*) earned far more royalties from her iconic bathing suit poster (which has sold more than 20 million copies) than from *Charlie's Angels*.

0296.
Actor and dancer Patrick Swayze (*Dirty Dancing, Ghost*) was an accomplished ice skater and gymnast.

0297.
Actor Paul Newman (*Cool Hand Luke, The Color of Money*) was an ordained minister.

0298.
Singer and actor Jon Bon Jovi (*Bon Jovi, U-571, Ally McBeal*) made his first commercial recording on *The Star Wars Christmas Album* in 1980. He sang a song called *R2-D2, We Wish You a Merry Christmas* under the credit John Bongiovi

0299.
Arnold Schwarzenegger (actor, bodybuilder, governor) was born in Austria in 1947. His father served in Hitler's Army.

0300.
Country music sweetheart Miranda Lambert has done a little bit of acting, too. She appeared on an episode of *Law and Order: Special Victims Unit.*

0301.
Actor Clint Eastwood made an awful lot of movies, and is arguably the second most famous movie cowboy of all time (after John Wayne). You might be surprised to find, then, that his very first movie role was as a geeky lab assistant, in 1955's *The Revenge of the Creature.*

0302.
It's hard to imagine Hollywood legend Al Pacino as anything other than highly successful. After all, he's made several award winning movies, been a big star on Broadway, and is still one of Hollywood's most sought after actors. But it wasn't always that way. When he was young, Pacino worked jobs as a janitor and a busboy.

0303.

Benjamin Franklin wanted the turkey to be the national bird of the United States. He thought it was more noble than the bald eagle.

0304.

Actor Sam Shepard (*The Right Stuff, Klondike*) is also an award winning playwright. He received a Pulitzer Prize for *Buried Child*, a play he wrote in 1979.

0305.

It's a good thing actor Woody Harrelson (*Cheers, White Men Can't Jump*) didn't turn out like his father. His father was a hit man who served life in prison for killing a federal judge.

0306.

The last person Marilyn Monroe called before she died was President John F. Kennedy. It is unknown whether he took her call.

0307.

Actor and musician Ozzy Osbourne is a member of the Church of England and says a prayer before each of his concerts.

0308.

Actor Tom Cruise (*Outsiders, Taps, Mission: Impossible*) once dated singer and actress *Cher*.

0309.

Actor Kevin Bacon is a Hollywood success story, still sought out for leading actor roles in movies. But who knew he had a key role in the horror classic *Friday the 13th*? We sure didn't.

0310.

Actor and producer Ashton Kutcher (*That '70s Show, Two and a Half Men*) was once convicted of burglary and served three years' probation.

0311.

Actor and director Alan Alda (*M*A*S*H, The West Wing*) also appeared extensively on Broadway, and is an Emmy Award winner.

0312.

Silent screen actor Charlie Chaplin is viewed today as a charming and beloved part of American film history. But in his day he was quite controversial, for his affection of very young women. At one point he was forced to leave the United States and moved to Switzerland.

0313.

At six feet tall, George Washington towered over most of his peers. People were a bit smaller in the 1700s.

0314.

Ever come across a gospel album titled *Katy Hudson*? It was released in 2001 to little fanfare. If you happen to have such an album, take a good look at the young lady on the cover. She may look familiar to you. Her name is Katheryn Elizabeth Hudson. More commonly known as Katy Perry.

0315.

Rock and roll megastars *The Beatles* are known pretty much all over the world. It helps to have great music attached to a catchy name. But *The Beatles* wasn't the band's first choice for a name. They tried *The Beatals*, and *The Silver Beetles*. We think they made the best choice.

0316.

Actor, director and producer Denzel Washington's son John once played professional football for the St. Louis Rams.

0317.

Actor Nicolas Cage (*Con-Air, Raising Arizona*) has played some pretty shady characters in movie roles, but it turns out he's a pretty nice guy. For example, he donated one million dollars to help the victims of Hurricane Katrina.

0318.

Actor George Clooney was an athlete in high school, and a pretty good baseball player. In 1977 he tried to go pro, and tried out for the Cincinnati Reds. He didn't make the cut.

0319.
Actor Alan Alda (*M*A*S*H, Paper Lion*) is the only person to win Emmy awards for acting, writing and directing the same series (*M*A*S*H*).

0320.
Actress Jamie Lee Curtis (*Halloween, True Lies*) patented her own invention, a better baby diaper, in 1987.

0321.
Colombian singer, dancer and model Shakira is also an accomplished poet. She wrote her first poem, called *La Rosa De Cristal (The Crystal Rose)* at the tender age of four.

0322.
We'll bet you a nickel you don't know who Robert Matthew Van Winkle is. Would you believe it's Vanilla Ice's real name?

0323.
After she was injured doing yoga, race car driver Danika Patrick fell in love with her physical therapist. She later married him.

0324.
Conservative talk show host Bill O'Reilly (*The O'Reilly Factor*) was the goalie on his high school hockey team.

0325.
Former game show host Bob Barker (*Truth of Consequences, The Price is Right*) holds the record as the oldest man to host a daytime game show. He was 83 when he retired.

0326.
Actress and model Scarlett Johansson (*North, Lost in Translation*) made her film debut at the tender age of nine, as John Ritter's daughter in the comedy *North*.

0327.
Beauty Eva Longoria (*Young and the Restless, Desperate Housewives*) founded a charity called Eva's Heroes, which helps developmentally disabled children.

0328.
Peter Gene Hernandez, better known as singer Bruno Mars, was born in Honolulu, Hawaii and raised in Waikiki. Lucky guy…

0329.
Roger Staubach, legendary quarterback of the Dallas Cowboys, was the first man to win both the Heisman and Super Bowl MVP award.

0330.
Sharon Osbourne (*The Osbournes, America's Got Talent, The Talk*) is a beautiful woman, and is one of the few celebrities who freely admits she's had plastic surgery.

0331.

The hairstyle actress Jennifer Aniston wore on the series *Friends* is still one of the most popular styles among American women. Stylists all over the country have women come in asking simply for "the Rachel." Even though the style was and is very popular, Anniston has been quoted as saying she hated it.

0332.

Pop star actress Selena Gomez established her own production company, July Moon Productions, at the tender age of sixteen.

0333.

Actor Tommy Lee Jones *(Lonesome Dove, Men in Black)* lives outside of San Antonio, Texas and speaks fluent Spanish.

0334.

Singer Beyonce Knowles, more commonly known simply as *Beyonce*, and singer and actress *Solange*, are sisters.

0335.

Actor Sean Penn *(Mystic River, Milk)* is better known for his tough guy or troubled guy roles than for his portrayal of sensitive and down home types. It might surprise you, then, to learn that his very first role in front of a camera was on the family friendly *Little House on the Prairie.*

0336.
Singing legend Bob Dylan broke his neck... literally, in a 1966 motorcycle accident. He shattered several vertebrae in his neck, and recovered fully, but still has neck pain from it.

0337.
Singer and *American Idol* winner Carrie Underwood is an actress too. She once appeared on an episode of *How I Met Your Mother*, and did the voice of a character named *Carrie Underworm* for a *Sesame Street* episode.

0338.
Actor Brad Pitt (*Ocean's Eleven, Fight Club*) is an amateur architect, and has been involved in organizations that design safe and reasonably prices housing for the poor.

0339.
Actor Bob Crane was most famous for playing Colonel Robert Hogan on *Hogan's Heroes.* Hogan was a fictional Air Force officer, but Crane was a real life veteran. He served in the National Guard from 1948 to 1950.

0340.
Hollywood beauty Jessica Alba (*Dark Angel, Fantastic Four*) says she suffered from Obsessive Compulsive Disorder as a child. But she's over it now. Now things all line up quite nicely.

0341.
Pop star singer, songwriter and actress Christina Aguilera said blues great Etta James was her musical influence. At James' funeral, Aguilera was asked to sing *At Last*, a song James made famous.

0342.
Actor Bob Crane was most famous for playing Colonel Robert Hogan on *Hogan's Heroes.* Apparently he liked being on film. He had a very bad habit of secretly videotaping his sexual exploits with the women he dated.

0343.
Terry Bradshaw was the number one pick in the overall draft in 1970. He went to the Pittsburgh Steelers because of a coin toss. The Steelers and Chicago Bears tied with the worst record the previous season (1-13), and flipped a coin to see who got first pick. If the Bears had won, Bradshaw would have played for Chicago.

0344.
Actress and model Emma Watson (*Harry Potter, The Bling Thing*) was only nine years old when the *Harry Potter* series started. In addition to acting she attended school on the set for five hours a day. She was a straight "A" student.

0345.
Author Darrell Maloney (*The Secession of Texas, Countdown to the Apocalypse*) was once the food and beverage manager at Turner Field in Atlanta, home of the Atlanta Braves baseball team.

0346.
Country music singer Shania Twain (*Whose Bed Have Your Boots Been Under?* and *The Woman in Me*) is part Native American. Her biological father traced his roots to the Cree Indian tribe. She is also a hunter and avid outdoorsman. Or is that outdoorswoman?

0347.
Actor Audie Murphy (*To Hell and Back, Whispering Smith*) was also an accomplished singer and songwriter.

0348.
Singer Marilyn Manson is a distant relative of conservative commentator Pat Buchanan.

0349.
Legendary Dallas Cowboys football coach Tom Landry was a war hero. He piloted B-17 bombers during the Second World War.

0350.
Actor Christopher Plummer (*The Sound of Music, The Man Who Would be King*) is a direct descendent of Canadian Prime Minister John Abbott.

0351.
Martial artist and actor Bruce Lee had five different names over the course of his lifetime. He was born Lee Jun-fan, later changed to Bruce Lee. He also had three Chinese names: Li Yuanxin, Li Xiaolong and Li Yuanjian.

0352.

Ed McMahon is best known as Johnny Carson's sidekick on *The Tonight Show*. But he had many other pursuits prior to that, including being a pitchman for vegetable slicers, a Bingo caller and a carnival barker.

0353.

Former Denver Broncos quarterback and Hall of Famer John Elway is one of Denver's most loved people. It seems he's become almost a part of the city. But he almost wasn't. He was originally drafted by the Baltimore Colts and then traded to Denver.

0354.

Roy Rogers, the cowboy movie star, adopted that name early in his career. His real name was Leonard Slye.

0355.

Actor Nick Nolte has had many memorable roles over the years (*The Prince of Tides, Cape Fear, The Deep, 48 Hrs.*) He was also a very talented athlete, lettering in three sports at Iowa State University.

0356.

Actress and model Ashley Greene, who played Alice Cullen in *Twilight*, continues to be plagued by a youthful mistake. Early in her career, she took a series of nude "selfies," which were loaded onto the internet without her permission. Despite several years of legal wrangling, they're still floating around the web. A cautionary tale for other young actresses…

0357.
Buddy Holly's classic rock and roll hit *Peggy Sue* was originally called "Cindy Lou," after Buddy's niece. He changed it as a favor for a friend.

0358.
Actor, director, writer, songwriter, and country music singer Kevin Costner is obviously a very talented man. But by far his biggest achievement (at least in our view) is that he once dated supermodel Elle Macpherson. Some guys have all the luck.

0359.
The grave of William H. Bonney, more commonly known as Billy the Kid, is surrounded by a wrought iron fence. That's not to keep his ghost in. It's to protect his gravestone. The first two markers on the grave were stolen and recovered in Granbury, Texas and Huntington Beach, California.

0360.
When singer Madonna was twenty, she dropped out of college and moved to New York City with nothing but the clothes on her back and $35 in her pocket. She has since called the move "the bravest thing I've ever done."

0361.
General Douglas MacArthur retired from the Army in 1937. Then World War Two happened, and he was recalled to active duty.

0362.
Country singer Charley Pride has always loved baseball, and played in his younger days. He's a bit too seasoned to do that these days, so he settles for being a part owner of the Texas Rangers.

0363.
Two new species of ferns, *G. germanotta* and *G. monstraparva* have been named in honor of singer Lady Gaga. Really.

0364.
Joe Namath is probably the best known New York Jet of all time. He also received offers to play for several major league baseball teams, including the Yankees, Pirates and Phillies.

0365.
Rapper and actor Eminem was arrested when he was twenty years old for a drive by shooting – with a paintball gun.

0366.
In 2008, actor and comedian Billy Crystal (*When Harry Met Sally, City Slickers, Soap*) signed a contract to play with the New York Yankees, for only one day. He played against the Pittsburgh Pirates as the designated hitter, and struck out.

0367.
Actress and producer Julia Roberts (*Pretty Woman, Steel Magnolias, Erin Brockovich*) wanted to be a veterinarian as a child.

0368.

Actor and comedian Robin Williams (*Mork and Mindy, Good Morning Vietnam, Mrs. Doubtfire*) is the great great grandson of former Mississippi Governor Anselm McLaurin.

0369.

Actor Josh Brolin has made some really memorable movies lately (*No Country for Old Men, American Gangster, True Grit, Men in Black 3*). We're sure that his step-mother, Barbra Streisand, is very proud of him.

0370.

Most of us have seen old black and white movies starring pint-sized sweetheart Shirley Temple. She was the darling of the industry in her day, winning the hearts of fans around the world. But did you know that a grown up Shirley Temple later became the U.S. Ambassador to Czechoslovakia?

0371.

Actress Ashley Judd (*Double Jeopardy, Norma Jean and Marilyn, Kiss the Girls*) once worked as a model in Japan.

0372.

Actor Michael Clarke Duncan (*Armageddon, The Green Mile*) once dug ditches for a Chicago gas company and was a bouncer for several Chicago night clubs.

0373.

Actor Patrick Swayze (*Dirty Dancing, Ghost*) studied classical ballet at the Harkness Ballet Academy.

0374.
Actor Kurt Russell (*Swing Shift, Overboard*) is the son of Neil Oliver Russell, who played Deputy Clem Foster in *Bonanza.*

0375.
Actress Farrah Fawcett (*Charlie's Angels, The Burning Bed*) is the most remembered cast member of *Charlie's Angels,* which is surprising because she quit after just one season.

0376.
Offered special duty in the Army after he was drafted, Elvis Presley turned it down. He said, "I don't want to be treated any different than anybody else. The Army can do whatever it wants with me."

0377.
Because of his opposition to the Vietnam War, actor Paul Newman (*Cool Hand Luke, The Color of Money*) was placed nineteenth on President Richard Nixon's infamous enemies list. Newman later called it his "greatest accomplishment."

0378.
Actress and model Emma Watson (*Harry Potter, The Bling Thing*) is as British as can be. But she attended college in the United States, at Brown College in Rhode Island.

0379.
Actor Denzel Washington (*Remember the Titans, Hurricane*) once considered becoming a preacher.

0380.
Katy Perry was born Katheryn Elizabeth Hudson. When her singing career started to take off, she decided to use her mother's maiden name of Perry, so she wouldn't be confused with actress *Kate Hudson.*

0381.
Pop sensation Ariana Grande (*Victorious*) is an actress, a singer, and the object of affection for countless American teenaged boys. She's also a vegan.

0382.
Director and actor Nicolas Cage (*Raising Arizona, Con-Air*) once owned his own castle in Germany.

0383.
Legendary singer and actress Rosemary Clooney, a darling of 20th century Hollywood musicals, was actor George Clooney's aunt.

0384.
Actor, director and writer Tom Hanks (*A League of their Own, Forrest Gump, The Green Mile*) is a major success these days, but he has said that his school days were something less than that. He described himself as a "painfully shy geek."

0385.
Actor Alan Alda (*M*A*S*H, Paper Lion*) is the only character who appeared in all 251 episodes of M*A*S*H*.

0386.
Arnold Schwarzenegger (actor, bodybuilder, governor) was largely ignored by his father, who favored his older brother Meinhard. His father believed that Arnold was not his biological son.

0387.
Actor and musician Ozzy Osbourne has been a presence on television for so long that many people don't realize he started out as a member of the rock band *Black Sabbath* in the 1970s.

0388.
Actor Sam Shepard (*The Right Stuff, Klondike*) wrote a science fiction play called *The Unseen Hand,* which influenced Richard O'Brien's musical *The Rocky Horror Show.*

0389.
Actor Woody Harrelson (*Cheers, White Men Can't Jump*) once worked as a woodcarver at King's Island amusement park. Hence the nickname.

0390.
Actor Dennis Quaid (*The Right Stuff, The Rookie, Wyatt Earp*) is a distant relative of western movie actor and singer Gene Autry.

0391.
All Dallas Cowboys fans, past and present, know who Roger Staubach is. After all, he was only the Cowboys' starting quarterback for four years, and won Super Bowls in two of them. Did you know he was also a Navy officer and saw combat in Vietnam?

0392.
Actor and producer Ashton Kutcher (*That '70s Show, Two and a Half Men*) once sold his blood to help pay his way through college at the University of Iowa.

0393.
Singer and actor Jon Bon Jovi (*Bon Jovi, U-571, Ally McBeal*) can thank his mom for his good looks. Her name is Carol Sharkey and she is a former Playboy Bunny.

0394.
British actor Daniel Radcliffe (*Harry Potter*) almost didn't get a chance to audition for the role of Harry Potter. His parents heard that all seven films would be filmed in Los Angeles, so they didn't tell him. He found out anyway. And the rest, as they say, is history.

0395.
Actress Jamie Lee Curtis (*Halloween, True Lies*) is actor Jake Gyllenhaal's godmother.

0396.

Most people view George Washington as a professional politician. But first he was a farmer, growing tobacco and then wheat.

0397.

Rapper Vanilla Ice (*Ice Ice Baby*) has never known his biological father. He got his name (Van Winkle) from the man his mother was married to when he was born.

0398.

Jeff Probst, host of the popular television show *Survivor*, once became romantically involved with one of the show's contestants (Julie Berry, *Survivor: Vanuatu*). They broke up four years later.

0399.

Conservative talk show host Bill O'Reilly (*The O'Reilly Factor*) met singer Billy Joel in high school. He later referred to Joel as a "hoodlum."

0400.

Former game show host Bob Barker (*Truth of Consequences, The Price is Right*) once appeared in an episode of *Bonanza*, as a character named "Mort."

0401.

Actress and model Scarlett Johansson (*North, Lost in Translation*) did all of her own stunts in *Iron Man 2*.

0402.
Beauty Eva Longoria (*Young and the Restless, Desperate Housewives*) has been able to trace her Spanish ancestry all the way back to the year 1592.

0403.
Peter Gene Hernandez, better known as singer Bruno Mars, was given the nickname at the age of two because of his resemblance to legendary wrestler Bruno Sammartino.

0404.
Sharon Osbourne (*The Osbournes, America's Got Talent, The Talk*) and husband Ozzy had to flee their home in 2005 when it caught fire and was badly damaged. The pair was treated for smoke inhalation but fully recovered.

0405.
In 1978 singing legend Bob Dylan became a born again Christian and released two albums of gospel music.

0406.
The popular term "bootylicious," which was recently added to the *Oxford English Dictionary*, was originally created to describe singer Beyonce Knowles, more commonly known simply as *Beyonce*.

0407.
British actor Orlando Bloom (*Lord of the Rings, Pirates of the Caribbean*) is a practicing Buddhist.

0408.

It hasn't been that long ago, but many people aren't aware that actor Sean Penn (*Mystic River, Milk*) was once married to Madonna.

0409.

Actor Brad Pitt (*Ocean's Eleven, Fight Club*) founded an organization called the *Make it Right Foundation* after Hurricane Katrina ravaged New Orleans. The organization built 150 new homes for hurricane victims.

0410.

Singer and *American Idol* winner Carrie Underwood is a *Walking Dead* fan. In fact, she recently told an interviewer she'd like to play a zombie in the show.

0411.

Actor Bob Crane was most famous for playing Colonel Robert Hogan on *Hogan's Heroes.* You might also remember a blonde who played a girl named Hilda on the show. Her real name was Patricia Olson, AKA Sigrid Valdis. She and Crane married, on the *Hogan's Heroes* set, in 1970.

0412.

Hollywood beauty Jessica Alba (*Dark Angel, Fantastic Four*) is smart too. She graduated from high school at the age of sixteen.

0413.
"Papa John" Schnatter, of *Papa John's Pizza* fame sold his 1971 Camaro to buy pizza ovens to start his business. He eventually made enough money to buy the car back.

0414.
Terry Bradshaw, former quarterback for the Pittsburgh Steelers and a sports announcer, was also good at throwing the javelin. In high school he set a national record by throwing it 245 feet.

0415.
Retired Atlanta Braves pitcher Tom Glavine had several twenty game seasons, won the Cy Young award twice, and had been inducted into the baseball Hall of Fame. But who knew that in high school he was also a very talented hockey player, and could have gone a completely different route. We're glad he chose baseball.

0416.
Actor Audie Murphy (*To Hell and Back, Whispering Smith*) was a successful actor and singer, as well as a beloved war hero. But he came from humble roots. He was born into a family of sharecroppers, and dropped out of fifth grade to pick cotton for the family.

0417.
Tonight Show host Jay Leno is dyslexic.

0418.
Comedian and actor Bob Hope is the only civilian to ever be awarded the United States Air Force's *Order of the Sword* in recognition to his years of supporting the military.

0419.
Country singer, actress, and beauty Faith Hill was adopted as an infant.

0420.
Country music singer Tim McGraw has said he might run for Governor of Tennessee some day.

0421.
Singer and actress Trisha Yearwood (*She's In Love With The Boy, Walk away Joe*) was a close friend of now-husband Garth Brooks long before either of them were famous.

0422.
Say what you will about singer Marilyn Manson, but he's a pretty smart guy. In college, he once aspired to be a journalist and wrote articles for a music magazine.

0423.
Ever heard of Alecia Beth Moore? No? Bet you've heard of singer and actress Pink, though, haven't you? They are one and the same.

0424.

Legendary Dallas Cowboys football coach Tom Landry wasn't just a football coach. He was also a comic book character, who appeared in comic books promoting Christianity.

0425.

Martial artist and actor Bruce Lee was an accomplished poet.

0426.

Ed McMahon is best known as Johnny Carson's sidekick on *The Tonight Show*. He was also a U.S. Marine Corps pilot. He was on his way to war with the Navy's Pacific Fleet when the bomb was dropped on Hiroshima. He was no longer needed and his orders were cancelled.

0427.

Former Denver Broncos quarterback and Hall of Famer John Elway is one of the best players the NFL has had. But he was also a good baseball player. In fact, the Kansas City Royals drafted Elway in 1979, but he chose to play football instead.

0428.

And, oh, by the way, That same year the Royals also drafted Miami Dolphins legend Dan Marino. Also as a pitcher.

0429.

Radio personality Howard Stern has had a rhinoplasty and liposuction (on his chin).

0430.
Actor Tommy Lee Jones *(Lonesome Dove, Men in Black)* looks most appropriate in a cowboy hat or a black suit. But he sometimes wears riding gear as well, since he's an avid polo player.

0431.
Actor Nick Nolte has had many memorable roles over the years *(The Prince of Tides, Cape Fear, The Deep, 48 Hrs.)* But few of us remember that he was also a male model.

0432.
Most of us have heard the story about actor and musician Ozzy Osbourne biting the head off a live bat during a 1982 concert. But did you know the bat bit him back, and he had to be treated for rabies?

0433.
Everyone knows Ben Franklin the politician. But he was also an inventor, who invented bifocal glasses and the lightning rod.

0434.
Famed home run hitter of the New York Yankees Babe Ruth wanted to get into sports broadcasting after he retired. But no one would hire him.

0435.
Director and producer Alfred Hitchcock is regarded as one of the best producers of horror films, even thirty years after his death. He had several phobias, including a life-long fear of policemen.

0436.
Actor Johnny Galecki (*Rosanne, The Big Bang Theory*) was originally asked to play the role of Sheldon in *The Big Bang Theory,* but felt he was better suited for the role of Leonard.

0437.
Actor, producer and director Philip Seymour Hoffman *(Twister, Almost Famous, Cold Mountain)* was a wrestler in high school, until a neck injury forced him to give up the sport.

0438.
Joe Namath is probably the best known New York Jet of all time. But he was also an actor who played in several movies. He also tried to be a game show host, but was beaten out for *Family Feud* by Ray Combs.

0439.
Country music legend Charley Pride's name was supposed to be Charl Frank Pride. But a clerk made an error on his birth certificate and typed Charley.

0440.

Hollywood sweetheart Shirley Temple wowed audiences in the 1930s and 40s. The tiny child could sing and dance and she made the whole world fall in love with her. But one of her best known performances was as an adult, with John Wayne, in *Fort Apache.*

0441.

Babe Ruth, the "Sultan of Swat," was best known, of course, for his home run record. But did you know he was also a very successful left handed pitcher in the first few years of his career?

0442.

Actress Michelle Rodriguez (*Girlfight, Fast and Furious*) is a beautiful woman with an equally beautiful first name: Mayte.

0443.

Actor Paul Walker (*Into the Blue, Joy Ride, Fast and Furious*) is best known for the *Fast and Furious* movies. But he made his bones on daytime TV, in the soap opera *The Young and the Restless.*

0444.

Actress Jordana Brewster (*The Faculty, Fast and Furious*) speaks fluent Portuguese.

0445.
Sixteenth President of the United States Abraham Lincoln suffered from clinical depression, although they didn't call it that back then. They called it "melancholy."

0446.
Rapper and actor Eminem was married and divorced from Kimberly Scott twice. They didn't try a third time.

0447.
Katy Perry is a beautiful woman indeed. In 2010 the readers of *Maxim* magazine voted her the most beautiful woman in the world.

0448.
Country music star Shania Twain never had it easy, growing up in poverty and roughing it as a child. When her mother and stepfather were killed in a terrible car accident in 1987, she went back home to care for her siblings. She played her songs at night to earn money to feed them.

0449.
Actress and producer Julia Roberts (*Pretty Woman, Steel Magnolias, Erin Brockovich*) plays the clarinet.

0450.
Elvis Presley studied karate, and even included karate kicks and moves in some of his on-stage performances.

0451.

Actor Josh Brolin (*No Country for Old Men, American Gangster, True Grit, Men in Black 3*) auditioned for the role of Batman, but the role was given to Ben Affleck instead.

0452.

Actress Ashley Judd (*Double Jeopardy, Norma Jean and Marilyn, Kiss the Girls*) also appeared in *Natural Born Killers*, but her scenes were cut before the film was released.

0453.

Pop sensation Ariana Grande (*Victorious*) was raised a catholic, but withdrew from the church out of protest after Pope Benedict labeled working women sinners.

0454.

How'd you like to have actress and model Cindy Crawford for a next door neighbor? Actor George Clooney does. Actually, that's a pretty good thing for her too. The two own side by side villas in Los Cabos, Mexico.

0455.

Actor, director and writer Tom Hanks (*A League of their Own, Forrest Gump, The Green Mile*) has played more memorable roles than we can count. But who remembers when he played one of Fonzie's buddies in *Happy Days*?

0456.
Actor Michael Clarke Duncan (*Armageddon, The Green Mile*) once stole a baseball bat from the dugout at Comiskey Park in Chicago.

0457.
Actor and comedian Robin Williams (*Mork and Mindy, Good Morning Vietnam, Mrs. Doubtfire*) is a video game junkie. He even named two of his children, Zelda and Cody, after game characters.

0458.
Shakira fans will tell you that the Colombian singer has the voice of an angel, but apparently that wasn't always the case. She was once rejected during an audition for her school choir. The choir director said she "sounded like a goat."

0459.
Actress Sally Field (*The Flying Nun, Smokey and the Bandit, Places in the Heart*) was a cheerleader in high school.

0460.
Actor Kurt Russell (*Swing Shift, Overboard*) played a jungle boy in an episode of *Gilligan's Island*. He was fourteen. Now, if a fourteen year old boy could figure out a way to get off the island, how come nobody else could?

0461.
Actress Farrah Fawcett (*Charlie's Angels, The Burning Bed*) died on June 25, 2009. Her death received very little press coverage, though, because pop singer Michael Jackson died the very same day.

0462.
Actor and dancer Patrick Swayze (*Dirty Dancing, Ghost*) bred Arabian horses.

0463.
Edward Lodewijk Van Halen, better known as Eddie Van Halen, was born in the Netherlands.

0464.
Singer and actor Jon Bon Jovi (*Bon Jovi, U-571, Ally McBeal*) was born John Francis Bongiovi, Jr. We're glad he shortened it.

0465.
Arnold Schwarzenegger (actor, bodybuilder, governor) lived in near poverty as a child. He has said that one of the highlights of his childhood was the day his family finally bought a refrigerator.

0466.
Actor and musician Ozzy Osbourne grew up struggling with a slew of medical issues, including dyslexia, attention deficit disorder and learning disabilities.

0467.

Actor Sam Shepard (*The Right Stuff, Klondike*) plays the banjo.

0468.

Actor Woody Harrelson (*Cheers, White Men Can't Jump*) once got married in Tijuana, Mexico. They intended to divorce the next day, but the office was closed. They had to return ten months later to divorce.

0469.

Actor Dennis Quaid (*The Right Stuff, The Rookie, Wyatt Earp*) once battled anorexia, but seems to have won the battle.

0470.

Actor and producer Ashton Kutcher (*That '70s Show, Two and a Half Men*) was the first Twitter user to have more than a million followers.

0471.

Actor Alan Alda (*M*A*S*H, Paper Lion*) commuted from Los Angeles to his home in New Jersey every weekend for eleven years while doing M*A*S*H.

0472.

British actor Daniel Radcliffe (*Harry Potter*) struggles with a neurological disorder that sometimes makes it difficult to write or tie his own shoes.

0473.
Actress Jamie Lee Curtis (*Halloween, True Lies*) has beaten two separate addictions, one for alcohol and the other for pain killers. She has said that recovery was the greatest achievement of her life.

0474.
George Washington had many hobbies, including fox-hunting, cockfighting and playing cards.

0475.
Rapper Vanilla Ice (*Ice Ice Baby*) received his nickname at age fourteen. He was the only white kid in a group of African Americans that he hung out with. They called him "Vanilla."

0476.
Actor Peter Fonda (*Easy Rider*) accidentally shot himself in the stomach when he was eleven years old and almost died.

0477.
Jeff Probst, host of the popular television show *Survivor,* is step father to two of actor Mark-Paul Gosselaar's children.

0478.
Conservative talk show host Bill O'Reilly (*The O'Reilly Factor*) was once a semi-pro pitcher for the *New York Monarchs.*

0479.
Comedian and actor Jeff Foxworthy is no dumb redneck. He once worked for IBM working on mainframe computers.

0480.
Actress and model Scarlett Johansson (*North, Lost in Translation*) can sing too. She released her first album, called *Anywhere I Lay My Head* in 2008.

0481.
Beauty Eva Longoria (*Young and the Restless, Desperate Housewives*) is genetically related to Chinese cellist Yo-Yo Ma.

0482.
Peter Gene Hernandez, better known as singer Bruno Mars, started performing at an early age. By four, he was famous on the island of Oahu for his impersonation of Elvis Presley.

0483.
In *The Falcon and the Snowman,* actor Sean Penn played a drug dealer named Andrew Daulton Lee. The film was based on a true story, and Penn later hired Lee as a personal assistant to help in his rehabilitation.

0484.
Actor Nicolas Cage once owned the LaLaurie Mansion in the French Quarter of New Orleans. It's been called "the most haunted house in America."

0485.

Controversial baseball slugger Barry Bonds (*Pittsburgh Pirates, San Francisco Giants*) is a hero to some, for breaking Hank Aaron's home run record, and an anti-hero to others, for being implicated in the scandal involving banned substances. Did you know that the Giants originally drafted him out of high school in 1982? They couldn't come to terms, though, so he went to college instead.

0486.

Singer and *American Idol* winner Carrie Underwood is an animal lover and a vegan. She stopped eating meat as a teenager because she said eating meat made her feel like she was eating one of her own pets.

0487.

Actor Bob Crane was most famous for playing Colonel Robert Hogan on *Hogan's Heroes.* After his murder, he was buried twice. Originally buried at a church in Westwood, his widow Sigrid Valdis (Heidi from *Hogan's Heroes*) had him moved to another cemetery twenty five miles away.

0488.

Hollywood beauty Jessica Alba (*Dark Angel, Fantastic Four*) learned how to swim before she could walk.

0489.

Pittsburgh Steeler quarterback once threw a touchdown pass to Lynn Swann that sailed seventy yards. *In the air.*

0490.

Singer and actress Pink (*Lady Marmalade, Get This Party Started*) has a sultry, slightly raspy voice that drives boys nuts. Perhaps it traces its roots to Pink's childhood, when she suffered from asthma.

0491.

Actor Audie Murphy (*To Hell and Back, Whispering Smith*) was a war hero who suffered from post traumatic stress syndrome (PTSD). During one episode, he once held his wife at gunpoint.

0492.

Singer Marilyn Manson is also an accomplished painter and artist.

0493.

Charlie Manson was convicted of conspiracy to commit the murders of seven people in the infamous *Helter Skelter* murders (1969). His name wasn't always Charles Manson. Born to an unmarried sixteen year old girl in 1943, the name the hospital initially gave him was "No-Name Maddox."

0494.

Legendary Dallas Cowboys football coach Tom Landry once appeared on the TV show *To Tell The Truth*, pretending to be a catholic priest.

0495.

David Letterman, host of *The David Letterman Show*, recently surpassed Johnny Carson and became the longest serving late night talk show host in history, at 31 years and counting.

0496.

Ed McMahon is best known as Johnny Carson's sidekick on *The Tonight Show*. But you could also call him General McMahon, of the California Air National Guard.

0497.

Former Denver Broncos quarterback and Hall of Famer John Elway played at Stanford University, where he broke all kinds of records and impressed the nation. But he never took Stanford to a single bowl game.

0498.

Actress Anne Hathaway (*The Princess Diaries*) grew up in a strong Catholic family. When she was a girl, she wanted to grow up to be a nun.

0499.

Actor Nick Nolte (*The Prince of Tides, Cape Fear, The Deep, 48 Hrs.*) was convicted of selling counterfeit documents in 1965 and was sentenced to 45 years in prison. But the sentence was suspended.

0500.
British actor Orlando Bloom (*Lord of the Rings, Pirates of the Caribbean*) has a tattoo of the Elvish word "nine" on his right wrist.

0501.
Tonight Show host Jay Leno only sleeps four to five hours a night.

0502.
Comedian and actor Bob Hope is the only civilian to have an active United States Air Force aircraft named after him. The *Spirit of Bob Hope* is a C-17 Globemaster stationed at Pope AFB, North Carolina.

0503.
Canadian singer Celine Dion is the youngest of fourteen children.

0504.
Country singer, actress, and beauty Faith Hill's first public performance was at age seven.

0505.
Singer Janet Jackson was a child actress long before she became a pop sensation. She appeared in shows such as *Good Times* and *Fame*.

0506.
Babe Ruth, the "Sultan of Swat," spent much of his youth in a brutal "reformatory," an early form of prison for juvenile offenders.

0507.
Everyone knows Ben Franklin the politician. He was also a successful newspaper editor and printer. He printed some of the first currency used in the United States.

0508.
Joe Namath is probably the best known New York Jet of all time. His nickname was "Broadway Joe," but he made only one appearance on Broadway. He was a cast replacement in the production *The Caine Mutiny Court Martial.*

0509.
Country music legend Charley Pride once played baseball in the Negro League for the Louisville Clippers. Pride and another player were traded to the Birmingham Black Barons. For a team bus.

0510.
One of child actress Shirley Temple's best movies as an adult was the John Wayne classic *Fort Apache.* In the movie, she played actor John Agar's love interest. If you've seen the movie and were convinced that there was a certain spark between Temple and Agar, it shouldn't be a surprise. The two were married at the time.

0511.
Famed home run hitter of the New York Yankees Babe Ruth
Was only 53 when he died of cancer.

0512.
Director and producer Alfred Hitchcock is regarded as one of
the best producers of horror films, even thirty years after his
death. He tried to enlist to help England fight in World War
I, but they rejected him. They said he was too obese.

0513.
Actor Johnny Galecki (*Rosanne, The Big Bang Theory*) owns
a large ranch in the wine country of California. He makes his
own wine and even has a log cabin on the property.

0514.
Harrison Ford (*Star Wars, Indiana Jones*) is a former Boy
Scout, who achieved the rank of Life Scout.

0515.
Actor and comedian Robin Williams (*Mork and Mindy,
Good Morning Vietnam, Mrs. Doubtfire*) owns over fifty
bicycles.

0516.
Actor and director Jack Nicholson (*One Flew Over the
Coocoo's Nest, As Good As It Gets*) has been nominated for
an Academy Award in every decade from the 1960s to the
2000s.

0517.

Pop singer Katy Perry isn't just a talented singer. She's a darn good songwriter as well. She not only writes many of her own songs, but has also written songs that have been recorded by *Kelly Clarkson, Britney Spears, Selena Gomez, Jessie James* and others.

0518.

When actress and producer Julia Roberts (*Pretty Woman, Steel Magnolias, Erin Brockovich*) was born, Coretta Scott King, wife of Dr. Martin Luther King Jr.) paid the hospital bill.

0519.

In the 1980s, actor Josh Brolin (*No Country for Old Men, American Gangster, True Grit, Men in Black 3*) was a member of a punk rock band called *Rich Kids on LSD*.

0520.

Actor Nicolas Cage is the nephew of director Francis Ford Coppola and actress Talia Shire.

0521.

One of actor Jim Parsons' (*The Big Bang Theory*) ancestors was the noted French architect Louis-Francois Trouard (1729-1804)

0522.
We don't blame actor Josh Lucas for changing his name to something easier. He was born Joshua Lucas Easy Dent Maurer.

0523.
Actress Ashley Judd (*Double Jeopardy, Norma Jean and Marilyn, Kiss the Girls*) has no children. She has told the press, "It's unconscionable to breed, with the number of children starving to death in impoverished countries."

0524.
Actor George Clooney once had a Vietnamese pot-bellied pig for a pet. His name was Max.

0525.
Colombian singer, dancer and model Shakira has another talent that most people have never seen. She is a trained belly dancer.

0526.
Actress Sally Field (*Smokey and the Bandit, Places in the Heart*) was a singer too. She sang on the soundtrack for her breakthrough TV series *The Flying Nun.*

0527.
Actor, director and writer Tom Hanks (*A League of their Own, Forrest Gump, The Green Mile*) is a diabetic.

0528.
Elvis Presley once hit the stage with a Derringer pistol hidden in his right boot after receiving death threats.

0529.
Actor Kurt Russell (*Swing Shift, Overboard*) once played second base for a California Angels minor league team called the Bend Rainbows.

0530.
Only three people can officially brag that they've had more than a billion views on YouTube. That's right, billion with a "b." They are Shakira, Justin Bieber and Lady Gaga.

0531.
The red bathing suit worn by Actress Farrah Fawcett (*Charlie's Angels, The Burning Bed*) in her iconic poster now hangs in the Smithsonian Museum in Washington.

0532.
Actor and dancer Patrick Swayze (*Dirty Dancing, Ghost*) was a licensed pilot who crashed his Cessna in Prescott Valley, California in 2000. He walked away unharmed.

0533.
Actor and director Nicolas Cage likes nice things. We've already mentioned the castle he once owned in Bavaria and his haunted mansion in New Orleans. Did we forget to mention that he once owned nine Rolls Royce automobiles?

0534.
Country music mega star Faith Hill was adopted as an infant and given the name Audrey Faith Perry. She grew up in a small town named Star, Mississippi. Perhaps it was a sign of things to come.

0535.
Despite his critical acclaim and commercial success as a guitar player, performer Eddie Van Halen can't read music.

0536.
Singer and actor Jon Bon Jovi (*Bon Jovi, U-571, Ally McBeal*) named his band *Bon Jovi* in 1984. He almost named it *Johnny Electric.*

0537.
Arnold Schwarzenegger (actor, bodybuilder, governor) is a veteran. Well, sort of. He served in the Austrian Army. He once went AWOL to attend a bodybuilding competition and spent a week in a military prison.

0538.
Actor and musician Ozzy Osbourne once worked at a car factory as a horn tuner, and had another job at a slaughterhouse.

0539.
George Washington owned a distillery which produced several varieties of liquor.

0540.

Actor Woody Harrelson (*Cheers, White Men Can't Jump*) married the daughter of playwright Neil Simon in 1985. The marriage lasted ten months.

0541.

Actor Dennis Quaid (*The Right Stuff, The Rookie, Wyatt Earp*) once appeared in an episode of *SpongeBob Squarepants*. He played Mr. Krabs' grandfather.

0542.

Actor and director Kevin Costner (*Bull Durham, Field of Dreams, Dances With Wolves*) has a degree in marketing and finance from California State University at Fullerton.

0543.

Say what you will about Justin Bieber, but he does have some musical talent. He knows how to play the piano, drums, guitar and trumpet.

0544.

British actor Daniel Radcliffe (*Harry Potter*) is an atheist.

0545.

Actor Sam Shepard (*The Right Stuff, Klondike*) was most famous for his portrayal of Chuck Yeager, the test pilot who broke the sound barrier, in *The Right Stuff*. In real life, Shepard has a fear of flying.

0546.
Rapper Vanilla Ice (*Ice Ice Baby*) is a talented motocross rider. In the 1980s, he won three straight titles at the Grand National Championships in Dallas.

0547.
Jeff Probst, host of the popular television show *Survivor,* is an ordained minister.

0548.
Conservative talk show host Bill O'Reilly (*The O'Reilly Factor*) once taught history and English at a high school in Miami.

0549.
Comedian and actor Jeff Foxworthy has authored several books.

0550.
Actress and model Scarlett Johansson (*North, Lost in Translation*) sang *One Whole Hour* for the soundtrack of the film *Wretches and Jabberers.*

0551.
Actor Jake Gyllenhaal (*October Sky, The Day After Tomorrow*) came from a well to do family, but his parents insisted he have summer jobs like many of the other boys. So he worked as a lifeguard and a busboy.

0552.

Shania Twain, one of the most beautiful and successful women in country music, is a vegetarian.

0553.

You already knew that actor Peter Fonda's most memorable role was in *Easy Rider*. But did you also know that he co-wrote and produced it?

0554.

Peter Gene Hernandez, better known as singer Bruno Mars, started performing with his family's band, The Love Notes, at age three.

0555.

Sharon Osbourne (*The Osbournes, America's Got Talent, The Talk*) used to have a habit of putting her own excrement into Tiffany boxes and sending the boxes to people who she felt had wronged her or her family.

0556.

Actor and director Heath Ledger (*The Patriot, Dark Knight*) was an avid chess player, and was Western Australia's Junior Chess Champion when he was eleven years old.

0557.

Singer and *American Idol* winner Carrie Underwood was voted "World's Sexiest Vegetarian" by PETA twice, in 2005 and in 2007.

0558.

Actor Sean Penn directed Shania Twain's *Dance With the One Who Brought You* video.

0559.

Singer and actress Pink (*Lady Marmalade, Get This Party Started*) is a resounding success in her professional life. But singing wasn't her first choice of professions. As a child, she was an avid and talented gymnast, and aspired to join the Olympic gymnastics team.

0560.

Controversial baseball slugger Barry Bonds (*Pittsburgh Pirates, San Francisco Giants*) also played one season for the *Alaska Goldpanners,* in the *Alaska Baseball League.*

0561.

Actor and wrestler Dwayne Douglas Johnson, known professionally as *The Rock,* is of Black Nova Scotia (Canadian) and Samoan heritage.

0562.

Actress Michelle Rodriguez (*Girlfight, Fast and Furious*) was born in San Antonio with a Hispanic surname. But she doesn't come from Mexican heritage. Her parents are from the Dominican Republic and Puerto Rico.

0563.

Actress Jordana Brewster (*The Faculty, Fast and Furious*) is a Yale graduate with a degree in English.

0564.
Actor Paul Walker (*Into the Blue, Joy Ride, Fast and Furious*) was raised as a member of the Church of Jesus Christ of Latter-day Saints.

0565.
Sixteenth President of the United States Abraham Lincoln was once the Postmaster of New Salem, Illinois.

0566.
Actress Anne Hathaway (*The Princess Diaries*) once wanted to be a nun, until she found out her brother was gay. Having to choose between supporting the church, with its extreme anti-gay views, or her brother, she chose her brother.

0567.
Pittsburgh Steeler quarterback Terry Bradshaw donated all four of his Super Bowl rings to Louisiana Tech University, his alma mater.

0568.
Actor Audie Murphy (*To Hell and Back, Whispering Smith*) was once arrested and charged with attempted murder. He was acquitted of all charges.

0569.
Charlie Manson was convicted of conspiracy to commit the murders of seven people in the infamous *Helter Skelter* murders (1969). His father was African American, but there is no indication the two ever met.

0570.

Actress Helen Hunt (*Mad About You, Twister, As Good as it Gets*) knows how to ballet dance.

0571.

Actress Eliza Dushku (*Buffy the Vampire Slayer, Doll House*) also lends her voice to many popular video games.

0572.

Ed McMahon is best known as Jonny Carson's sidekick on *The Tonight Show*. He also had a bit part in the movie *The Incident* in 1967.

0573.

Before he ever played in the NFL, Former Denver Broncos quarterback and Hall of Famer John Elway played major league baseball. For the New York Yankees' farm team the Oneonta Yankees.

0574.

At the age of fifteen, British actor Orlando Bloom (*Lord of the Rings, Pirates of the Caribbean*) gave himself a tattoo, a sun, on his lower abdomen.

0575.

Dan Akroyd (*Saturday Night Live, Ghostbusters*) has one green eye and one brown eye.

0576.

Comedian and actor Bob Hope once owned part of the Cleveland Indians baseball team.

0577.

Canadian singer Celine Dion wrote her first song, *It Was Only a Dream,* at age twelve.

0578.

Dan Akroyd (*Saturday Night Live, Ghostbusters*) was born with webbed toes.

0579.

Everyone knows Ben Franklin the politician. But did you know that he also published the *Philadelphische Zeitung*? It was the first German-language newspaper in the United States.

0580.

As a convicted felon, actor Nick Nolte (*The Prince of Tides, Cape Fear, The Deep, 48 Hrs.*) was not eligible to join the military. He was upset about that. As thousands of young American men wanted to get out of going to Vietnam, Nolte actually wanted to go but couldn't.

0581.

Pop music beauty Avril Lavigne hails from Ontario and is a Canadian citizen. Most fans of her music know that. But not many know she also holds a dual citizenship with France.

0582.
Wrestling promoter Vince McMahon didn't meet his father until he was twelve years old.

0583.
Actor, model and former rapper Mark Wahlberg (AKA Marky Mark) is a distant relative of author Nathaniel Hawthorne.

0584.
In her younger days, country singer, actress, and beauty Faith Hill sold t-shirts for a living. She was also a secretary and worked at McDonald's.

0585.
Singer Janet Jackson was born Janet Damita Jo Jackson, the youngest of ten children.

0586.
Babe Ruth, the "Sultan of Swat," was lucky to be alive. Of eight children in the family, only he and a younger sister survived infancy.

0587.
Sixteenth President of the United States Abraham Lincoln told his wife Mary he wanted to visit the Holy Land. They were at Ford's theater, and he was assassinated within the hour.

0588.

Actor Jim Parsons estimates he auditioned for fifteen to thirty television pilots before *The Big Bang Theory*. That's a lot of auditions.

0589.

Director and producer Alfred Hitchcock was famous for making discrete appearances in many of his own movies. In the movie *Lifeboat*, which was shot mostly in a small boat, that was a problem. They solved the problem by placing Hitchcock's photograph in a newspaper that one of the men in the boat was reading.

0590.

Actress and singer Jennifer Lopez (*My Little Girl, In Living Color*) started singing and dancing lessons when she was only five years old.

0591.

Actor Joe Pesci (*Goodfellas, Casino, My Cousin Vinny*) can play the guitar, and once played in several bands.

0592.

Actress and producer Julia Roberts (*Pretty Woman, Steel Magnolias, Erin Brockovich*) once played in a movie with her brother, Eric Roberts. It was called *Blood Red*, and you've probably never heard of it.

0593.
Harrison Ford (*Star Wars, Indiana Jones*) also played a U.S. Army officer named G. Lucas in *Apocalypse Now.* It was a nod to his friend, director George Lucas.

0594.
Actor and director Jack Nicholson (*One Flew Over the Coocoo's Nest, As Good As It Gets*) grew up believing that his grandparents were his parents and that his mother was a sister.

0595.
Actress Sally Field (*The Flying Nun, Smokey and the Bandit, Places in the Heart*) once appeared in *Playboy* magazine. No, not really. But she really did appear on the cover once, in bunny ears.

0596.
Former soccer star David Beckham was the first player to win league titles in four different countries.

0597.
Colombian singer, dancer and model Shakira is fluent in Spanish, English, Portuguese, Italian and French. She also speaks "some Arabic."

0598.
Actress Anna Chlumsky (*My Girl, My Girl 2*) once aspired to be a paleontologist.

0599.
Actor Josh Lucas (*Sweet Home Alabama, A Beautiful Mind, Poseidon*) is a big supporter of Barack Obama. While campaigning for him, he once wore an Obama shirt for 45 consecutive days.

0600.
Actress Ashley Judd (*Double Jeopardy, Norma Jean and Marilyn, Kiss the Girls*) was awarded her bachelor's degree in French from the University of Kentucky, on the Ellen DeGeneres Show.

0601.
Elvis Presley was secretly photographed in his casket by one of his cousins. The photograph was sold to *The National Enquirer*, who put it on their cover. It was their best selling issue ever.

0602.
Actor Kurt Russell (*Swing Shift, Overboard*) used to be a pretty good ballplayer. Before a shoulder injury ended his career, he led the Texas League with a .563 batting average.

0603.
Actress Demi Moore (*St. Elmo's Fire, Indecent Proposal*) dropped out of high school at age sixteen.

0604.
The song *Midnight Train to Georgia* was inspired by actress Farrah Fawcett (*Charlie's Angels, The Burning Bed*) and actor Lee Majors (*The Six Million Dollar Man*)

0605.
Country music star Faith Hill formed her own band at age 17, and performed at local rodeos. She also went into the local jail to sing gospel songs to the prisoners.

0606.
Actor, director and writer Tom Hanks (*A League of their Own, Forrest Gump, The Green Mile*) once wanted to be an astronaut, but wasn't good enough in math.

0607.
It wasn't a big surprise that Peyton Manning (Denver Broncos) became a quarterback. It's a family tradition of sorts. His father, Archie Manning, played many years as quarterback for the New Orleans Saints.

0608.
Singer and guitar guru Eddie Van Halen has also been trained in classical piano.

0609.
Arnold Schwarzenegger (actor, bodybuilder, governor) won the title of Mr. Olympia seven times.

0610.
Singer and actor Jon Bon Jovi (*Bon Jovi, U-571, Ally McBeal*) generally supports politicians of the democratic party, and people assume he's a democrat himself. But according to his voter registration form, he's an independent.

0611.
Actor Woody Harrelson (*Cheers, White Men Can't Jump*) once owned an oxygen bar in Hollywood called "O2."

0612.
Actor Dennis Quaid (*The Right Stuff, The Rookie, Wyatt Earp*) is also a musician and has his own band, called *The Sharks.*

0613.
Actor Paul Walker (*Into the Blue, Joy Ride, Fast and Furious*) majored in marine biology in college.

0614.
Sixteenth President of the United States Abraham Lincoln was neither a Republican nor a Democrat. He was a member of the Whig Party.

0615.
Actress and singer Jennifer Lopez (*My Little Girl, In Living Color*) was a talented athlete in high school. She ran track on a national level and played on the school softball team.

0616.
Actor and musician Ozzy Osbourne can do many things well, but he's a lousy burglar. He once tried to steal a television, but it fell on him and he had to leave it behind.

0617.
Actor Sam Shepard (*The Right Stuff, Klondike*) has written several books of short stories and essays.

0618.
Actor and director Kevin Costner (*Bull Durham, Field of Dreams, Dances With Wolves*) sings in his own band, called *Kevin Costner and Modern West.*

0619.
Justin Bieber flew from Canada to Atlanta to record his first record at the tender age of thirteen.

0620.
British actor Daniel Radcliffe (*Harry Potter*) is the only non-royal ever to have his individual portrait hung in Britain's National Portrait Gallery.

0621.
Actor Jake Gyllenhaal (*October Sky, The Day After Tomorrow*) is a direct descendent of Swedish nobility.

0622.

On the day George Washington died, his doctors drained much of his blood, a practice then known as "bloodletting." It's been estimated that they may have removed as much as half of the blood in his body. Some modern medical experts believe his own doctors may have inadvertently killed him.

0623.

Rapper Vanilla Ice (*Ice Ice Baby*) was stabbed five times during a 1987 brawl at a night club in South Dallas.

0624.

Russell Brand reportedly told wife Katy Perry she was divorcing her via text message. Then, according to Perry, he never spoke to her again.

0625.

We already mentioned that Jeff Probst, host of the popular television show *Survivor,* is an ordained minister. Did we mention that he presided over the wedding of actress Jenna Fischer (*The Office*)?

0626.

While attending Boston University, conservative talk show host Bill O'Reilly (*The O'Reilly Factor*) met fellow student Howard Stern. He said he noticed Stern because he was the only student on campus taller than O'Reilly was.

0627.
Actress and model Scarlett Johansson (*North, Lost in Translation*) describes herself as Jewish, but she celebrates both Christmas and Hanukkah.

0628.
Sharon Osbourne (*The Osbournes, America's Got Talent, The Talk*) has said that the biggest mistake of her life was having an abortion at seventeen.

0629.
In 2011 actor Peter Fonda (*Easy Rider*) found the body of a man sitting in a car alongside Sunset Boulevard. The man had committed suicide three days before and no one noticed until Fonda decided to stop.

0630.
Actress Jennifer Lawrence (*The Hunger Games*) auditioned for a role in the original *Twilight* movie in 2007. She didn't get the part of Bella Swan, though. It went to another actress you may have heard of named Kristen Stewart.

0631.
Singer and actress Pink (*Lady Marmalade, Get This Party Started*) credited someone who might be considered as a bit unusual as her biggest musical influence: 1960s singer Janis Joplin.

0632.
Actor and wrestler Dwayne Douglas Johnson, known professionally as *The Rock,* played football at the *University of Miami* and was a member of the 1991 National Championship team.

0633.
Actress Michelle Rodriguez (*Girlfight, Fast and Furious*) dropped out of high school, but later earned her GED.

0634.
In 2005 actor Sean Penn (*Mystic River, Milk*) went to New Orleans to help rescue victims of Hurricane Katrina. Many other celebrities sent money, but Penn was actually helping pull people off of rooftops and into boats.

0635.
Bob Denver played Gilligan on *Gilligan's Island*, and that's how most of us remember him. But some also remember him from his days teaching math and physical education at an elementary school in Pacific Palisades, California.

0636.
Actress and singer Jennifer Lopez (*My Little Girl, In Living Color*) was a backup dancer for the 1990s boy band *New Kids on the Block.*

0637.
Actress Anne Hathaway (*The Princess Diaries*) is a vegan.

0638.
Controversial baseball slugger Barry Bonds (*Pittsburgh Pirates, San Francisco Giants*) graduated from Arizona State University in 1986. His degree? Criminology.

0639.
Hollywood beauty Jessica Alba (*Dark Angel, Fantastic Four*) is a Professional Association of Diving Instructors (PADI) – certified scuba diver.

0640.
British actor Orlando Bloom (*Lord of the Rings, Pirates of the Caribbean*) once slipped off a roof, fell three stories, and broke his back.

0641.
Actor and producer Johnny Depp (*Edward Scissorhands, Pirates of the Caribbean*) moved frequently in his youth. By the time he became an adult, he had lived in twenty different places.

0642.
Comedian and actor Bob Hope earned money starting at age twelve by singing and dancing on street cars in New York City.

0643.
Canadian singer Celine Dion met her husband when she was twelve and he was thirty eight.

0644.
Sixteenth President of the United States Abraham Lincoln left home when he was twenty two. He went to New Orleans, and was so disgusted by the treatment of slaves he saw there, he walked home. All the way back to Illinois.

0645.
Actress Susan Sarandon (*Dead Man Walking, The Great Waldo Pepper*) got her start in soap operas. She appeared in *A World Apart* and *Search for Tomorrow*).

0646.
Canadian pop star Avril Lavigne's middle name is Ramona.

0647.
In the early 1970s, professional football didn't pay very well. Not even to its superstar athletes. Pittsburgh Steeler quarterback Terry Bradshaw had to sell used cars on the side to supplement his income.

0648.
Actress Eliza Dushku (*Buffy the Vampire Slayer, Doll House*) is of Albanian descent. She has an Albanian eagle tattoo on the back of her neck.

0649.
Actor and director Jack Webb (*Dragnet*) was married to former Miss USA Jackie Loughery.

0650.
Ben Franklin had an illegitimate son named William.

0651.
Ed McMahon is best known as Jonny Carson's sidekick on *The Tonight Show.* But long before that he was a flight instructor in the United States Marine Corps.

0652.
Actress Helen Hunt (*Mad About You, Twister, As Good as it Gets)* had several TV roles as a child, including parts in *The Mary Tyler Moore Show* and *The Bionic Woman.*

0653.
Director Steven Spielberg (*E.T.-The Extra-Terrestrial, Jaws*) was an Eagle Scout in high school.

0654.
Pittsburgh Steeler quarterback Ben Roethlisberger has said the reason he chose number 7 for his uniform was because he grew up idolizing John Elway.

0655.
The infamous mug shot of actor Nick Nolte (*The Prince of Tides, Cape Fear, The Deep, 48 Hrs.*)... the one with the dazed look and the unruly hair, wasn't a mug shot at all. It was taken at a hospital where he was taken to submit blood after a DUI arrest.

0656.
David Hasselhoff (*Baywatch, Knight Rider*) was nicknamed "Hooves" in high school.

0657.
Singer Janet Jackson was raised as a Jehovah's witness.

0658.
Actor, model and former rapper Mark Wahlberg (AKA Marky Mark) had a troubled childhood. He was in trouble with the Boston Police Department twenty times before the age of eighteen.

0659.
Actor, comedian and director Woody Allen was born in the Bronx in 1935. His birth name was Allan Stewart Konigsberg.

0660.
Famous college and professional football coach Bill Parcels (*Air Force Academy Falcons, New York Giants* and *Jets, New England Patriots, Dallas Cowboys*) is nicknamed the Big Tuna. Do you know where he got the nickname? It's because certain members of the Patriots thought his body was shaped like one.

0661.
Country music superstar Faith Hill once auditioned to be a backup singer for Reba McIntire, but didn't get the job.

0662.

Country singer, actress, and beauty Faith Hill had her acting debut on an episode of the family-friendly *Touched By An Angel*.

0663.

In 1988, actress Sally Field (*The Flying Nun, Smokey and the Bandit, Places in the Heart*) survived a plane crash. She escaped with only minor injuries.

0664.

Here's a shocker: Actor and director Jack Nicholson (*One Flew Over the Coocoo's Nest, As Good As It Gets*) was voted "class clown" in high school.

0665.

Actress and producer Julia Roberts (*Pretty Woman, Steel Magnolias, Erin Brockovich*) was offered the role of Annie Reed in *Sleepless in Seattle*, but she turned it down.

0665a.

Posh Spice (*The Spice Girls*) isn't just another pretty face and the wife of soccer legend David Beckham. She's also published two best-sellers.

0667.

Actress Demi Moore (*St. Elmo's Fire, Indecent Proposal*) made some great movies. But long before that, she was in the soap opera *General Hospital*.

0668.

Harrison Ford (*Star Wars, Indiana Jones*) is a talented carpenter. He was once hired to build cabinets at the home of director George Lucas. That led him into a more lucrative business.

0669.

Elvis Presley had an identical twin brother, Jesse Garon Presley, who was stillborn 35 minutes before Elvis was born.

0670.

Babe Ruth, the "Sultan of Swat," was also a talented carpenter.

0671.

Singer, songwriter and actress Pink (*Lady Marmalade, Get This Party Started*) was married to motocross racer Carey Hart in 2006. She proposed to him, in the middle of a race, using a pit board.

0672.

Actress Kaley Cuoco (*The Big Bang Theory*) started playing tennis at age three and was once a nationally ranked amateur.

0673.

Director and producer Alfred Hitchcock fell in love with the Pacific Ocean while filming *The Birds* in 1960. So much so, in fact, that he had his ashes scattered there after his death.

0674.
Actor Kurt Russell (*Swing Shift, Overboard*) provided the voice for Elvis Presley in the movie *Forrest Gump.*

0675.
Denver Broncos quarterback Peyton Manning owns 21 Papa John's Pizza franchises in Colorado.

0676.
Almost all of director and producer Alfred Hitchcock's heroines were blondes, as were most of his murder victims. But he never explained why.

0677.
Actor Alec Baldwin (*Hunt for Red October, The Aviator, 30 Rock*) started his acting career on a soap opera called *The Doctors.*

0678.
Actor Dennis Quaid (*The Right Stuff, The Rookie, Wyatt Earp*) is a five-handicap golfer.

0679.
Singer and guitar guru Eddie Van Halen owns three U.S. patents, for various guitar parts he developed.

0680.
Actress Debbie Reynolds was born on April first. And that's no joke…

0681.
Charlie Manson was convicted of conspiracy to commit the murders of seven people in the infamous *Helter Skelter* murders (1969). He once claimed his alcoholic mother traded him for a pitcher of beer.

0682.
You may not remember it, but singer and actor Jon Bon Jovi (*Bon Jovi, U-571, Ally McBeal*) had his first movie role in 1990. He played "the long haired corpse in the coffin."

0683.
Arnold Schwarzenegger (actor, bodybuilder, governor) was an illegal alien for a time in the late 1960s and early 1970s because of violations of the terms of his visa.

0684.
Elvis Presley's fans were way too devoted, even after his death. Several of them even tried to steal his body in September, 1977.

0685.
Actress and director Goldie Hawn (*Laugh-In, Private Benjamin, Best Friends*) is the mother of actress Kate Hudson.

0686.
Actor and musician Ozzy Osbourne once spent six weeks in prison for burglarizing a clothing store.

0687.
Actor Woody Harrelson (*Cheers, White Men Can't Jump*) Refuses to eat meat or dairy products. That's not uncommon. But he also refuses to eat flour or sugar.

0688.
Actor and director Jack Webb (*Dragnet*) never met his father.

0689.
Singer Kelly Clarkson, winner of the first *American Idol*, has said that her family struggled when she was a child. She found refuge in her music, which allowed her a chance to escape the grim realities of life.

0690.
Actor Jake Gyllenhaal (*October Sky, The Day After Tomorrow*) made his acting debut with Billy Crystal in *City Slickers*. He was the precocious kid who asked the Walker Brandt character if she really modeled ladies underwear.

0691.
George Washington, our first President, was a red head.

0692.

British actor Daniel Radcliffe (*Harry Potter*) writes poetry.

0693.

Rapper Vanilla Ice (*Ice Ice Baby*) once dated singer Madonna.

0694.

Former game show host Bob Barker (*Truth or Consequences, The Price is Right*) is a member of the Sioux tribe and grew up on an Indian reservation in South Dakota.

0695.

Sharon Osbourne (*The Osbournes, America's Got Talent, The Talk*) has said that her own father once robbed her and tried to kill her.

0696.

Actress and model Scarlett Johansson (*North, Lost in Translation*) hates the nickname "ScarJo" that the tabloids have given her. She calls it "awful" and "terrible."

0697.

Actor and wrestler Dwayne Douglas Johnson, known professionally as *The Rock,* once played professional football for the Calgary Stampeders of the Canadian Football League.

0698.
Actress Michelle Rodriguez (*Girlfight, Fast and Furious*) wasn't the best of students. She was expelled from five different schools.

0699.
Actor Paul Walker (*Into the Blue, Joy Ride, Fast and Furious*) was in a Pampers commercial as a baby and started modeling at age two.

0700.
Actress Susan Sarandon (*Bull Durham, Dead Man Walking*) was once an Olympic flag bearer.

0701.
Actress and comedian Lucille Ball's middle name was Desiree.

0702.
Singer, songwriter and actor Usher's real name is Usher Raymond IV.

0703.
Actress Amy Adams (*Man of Steel, American Hustle*) is legally an American, since both of her parents are American citizens. But she was actually born in Italy.

0704.

Actor Joe Pesci (*Goodfellas, Casino, My Cousin Vinny*) made the shortest acceptance speech in Oscar Awards history, with just five words: "It's my privilege. Thank you."

0705.

Singer and actor Clay Aikin (*American Idol*) has announced his intention to run for Congress in his native state of North Carolina.

0706.

Actor Ralph Macchio (*Karate Kid, My Cousin Vinny*) met his wife Phyllis, a nurse practitioner, when he was only fifteen. They are now happily married with two children.

0707.

Character actor Fred Gwynne (*The Munsters, My Cousin Vinny*) was best known as his role of Herman, a Frankenstein-like character in *The Munsters*. Many years before that, though, he was a cartoonist.

0708.

Controversial baseball slugger Barry Bonds (*Pittsburgh Pirates, San Francisco Giants*) was the first player in its thirty year history to resign from the Major League Baseball Player's Association's licensing agreement. He thought he could make more money selling his own merchandize. That's why you can't buy any of his memorabilia under the MLBPA brand.

0709.

Actor Tim Robbins' middle name is Francis.

0710.

Actor Sean Penn (*Mystic River, Milk*), and the late Hugo Chavez, President of Venezuela, were close personal friends.

0711.

Singer and *American Idol* winner Carrie Underwood was not only a cheerleader in high school. She was also her graduating class's salutatorian.

0712.

Bob Denver, who played Gilligan on *Gilligan's Island,* was once arrested for marijuana possession. He initially said that Dawn Wells, who played Mary Ann on the same show, gave it to him. But he refused to name her in court, took the rap, and served six months probation.

0713.

Hollywood beauty Jessica Alba (*Dark Angel, Fantastic Four*) once got into trouble with the law... for posting posters of sharks all over Oklahoma City

0714.

After actor and director Jack Webb (*Dragnet*) died in 1982, the Los Angeles Police Department retired his badge number 714.

0715.
Actor and producer Johnny Depp (*Edward Scissorhands, Pirates of the Caribbean*) still has scars he inflicted on himself as a troubled youth.

0716.
Comedian and actor Bob Hope was once a semi-professional boxer. He went by the name Packy East.

0717.
Ben Franklin invented a lot of things, but never patented any of them. He said he wanted people to have the opportunity to use them and improve upon them freely.

0718.
Canadian pop star Avril Lavigne (*Complicated, SK8R Boy*) has the reputation as being a bit of a rebel, and some of her songs have an edgy style that reflects that. But perhaps some of it is beyond her control. She has suffered from AD/HD since childhood and used to get in trouble in school because of it.

0719.
Actress Eliza Dushku (*Buffy the Vampire Slayer, Doll House*) holds dual citizenship in the United States and in Albania.

0720.
John Elway is the oldest player to score a touchdown in a Super Bowl. He was 38.

0721.
Comedian and actress Melissa McCarthy (*Gilmore Girls, Mike and Molly*) is also the cousin of comedian Jenny McCarthy.

0722.
Which musician sold more tickets and earned more money than any other act in the period from 2000 to 2010? *Madonna? Britney Spears? Michael Jackson?* Keep guessing. We'll take a nap and wait for you to get to the real answer, a young man by the name of Dave Matthews.

0723.
Ever heard of Robert Allen Zimmerman? No? We bet you've heard of Bob Dylan. It's the same guy.

0724.
Stefani Joanne Angelina Germanotta is quite a mouthful. No wonder she changed her name to Lady Gaga.

0725.
David Hasselhoff (*Baywatch, Knight Rider*) was a soap opera star before he broke into prime time. He played Dr. William Foster in *The Young and the Restless.*

0726.
Actor, comedian and director Woody Allen is also an accomplished musician. He plays the clarinet and has his own jazz band.

0727.
Famous college and professional football coach Bill Parcels was a gifted athlete himself. In high school he played football, baseball and basketball as a quarterback, pitcher and center.

0728.
Actor, director and writer Tom Hanks (*A League of their Own, Forrest Gump, The Green Mile*) is an honorary member of the U.S. Army Rangers Hall of Fame. He was given the honor for his role in *Saving Private Ryan.*

0729.
Singer Beyonce Knowles, better known as simply Beyonce, is more than just another pretty face and talented musician. In 2013, she was named as one of *Time* magazine's 100 most influential people in the world.

0730.
We don't know why actress Helen Hunt (*Mad About You, Twister, As Good as it Gets*) had a fascination with Hawaii. We couldn't find any indication she ever lived there. But she named her daughter Makena Lei. Maybe she just likes Hawaiian names.

0731.
Sultry R&B singer and actress Alicia Keys once won five Grammy awards in a single night.

0732.
Actor, model and former rapper Mark Wahlberg (AKA Marky Mark) was once charged with two counts of attempted murder, but plead guilty to assault. He served 45 days of a two year sentence.

0733.
Actor and director Jack Nicholson (*One Flew Over the Coocoo's Nest, As Good As It Gets*) wasn't the best high school student. He was in detention every single day of one school year.

0734.
Actress and producer Julia Roberts (*Pretty Woman, Steel Magnolias, Erin Brockovich*) practices Hinduism.

0735.
Actress and producer Kristen Bell (*Veronica Mars, When in Rome*) also provides the face and voice for a series of video games called *Assassin's Creed.*

0736.
Venerable actor Morgan Freeman (*Driving Miss Daisy, Shawshank Redemption, Bruce Almighty*) is a military veteran. He served in the United States Air Force as a radar technician.

0737.

Harrison Ford (*Star Wars, Indiana Jones*) got the scar on his chin when he ran his car into a telephone pole at age twenty two.

0738.

Elvis Presley was part Cherokee Indian, on his mother's side.

0739.

Country music singer Tim McGraw is the son of the late major league baseball player Tug McGraw.

0740.

When she was eight years old, singer Janet Jackson was instructed not to call her father "Dad" any more. He was her manager, and she was to call him "Joseph."

0741.

Actress Demi Moore (*St. Elmo's Fire, Indecent Proposal*) was cross-eyed as a child.

0742.

Actor Kurt Russell (*Swing Shift, Overboard*) is a licensed pilot.

0743.

Actor Alec Baldwin (*Hunt for red October, The Aviator, 30 Rock*) used to be a bus boy at Studio 54 in New York City.

0744.
Denver Broncos (and former Tennessee Volunteers) quarterback Peyton Manning once threw five touchdown passes against Texas Tech University.

0745.
Actor Paul Newman (*Cool Hand Luke, The Color of Money*) founded Newman's Own food company. All profits from the company were donated to charity. Newman died in 2008, but Newman's Own lives on.

0746.
Famed home run hitter of the New York Yankees Babe Ruth learned how to sew while at a youth reformatory. Even as a highly paid athlete many years later, he altered his own clothes to fit him better.

0747.
Director and producer Alfred Hitchcock appeared briefly in nearly all of his films.

0748.
Actress Kaley Cuoco (*The Big Bang Theory*) once played *Brady Bunch* actress Maureen McCormick in a TV movie called *Growing Up Brady*.

0749.
Radio personality Howard Stern is a talented photographer. His photos have been published in several magazines.

0750.

Actor Dennis Quaid (*The Right Stuff, The Rookie, Wyatt Earp*) is a licensed pilot.

0751.

Arnold Schwarzenegger (actor, bodybuilder, governor) once dead lifted 710 pounds. That's more than you and your next door neighbor combined.

0752.

Comedian and actress Ellen DeGeneres (*Mr. Wrong, Finding Nemo, The Ellen DeGeneres Show*) once worked at J.C. Penny and waited tables at a T.G.I. Friday's.

0753.

Actor and musician Ozzy Osbourne once witnessed a plane crash that killed his good friend and band mate Randy Rhodes. The plane was buzzing Osbourne's bus when it crashed.

0754.

Steven Speilberg, considered one of the most influential Hollywood screen directors of all time, has produced too many blockbusters to mention (*Jaws, E.T., Jurassic Park, Schindler's List,* just to name a few). But he wasn't always so respected. He was terribly bullied in high school by anti-Semitics and beaten up many times.

0755.
Actress and director Goldie Hawn (*Laugh-In, Private Benjamin, Best Friends*) is a direct descendent of Edward Rutledge, who signed the Declaration of Independence.

0756.
Charlie Manson was convicted of conspiracy to commit the murders of seven people in the infamous *Helter Skelter* murders (1969). He's had several names over the course of his lifetime, including No-Name Maddox and Charles Milles Maddox. These days he resides at Corcoran State Prison, and his name is Inmate B-33920.

0757.
Dallas Cowboys football coach Tom Landry has been gone for awhile now, having died in 2000. But he still holds several distinctive records. For example, he is the only man in NFL history who has coached the same team for 29 years.

0758.
Actor Woody Harrelson (*Cheers, White Men Can't Jump*) did not really eat Twinkies in the movie *Zombieland.* They were fake Twinkies, made with corn meal.

0759.
Actor and director Jack Webb (*Dragnet*) wanted to be a pilot during World War II, so he joined the Army Air Corps. But he washed out of flight training.

0760.
Singer Kelly Clarkson, the winner of the first *American Idol*, toyed with acting early in her career. She made several appearances on the television shows *Dharma and Greg* and *Sabrina the Teenage Witch.*

0761.
British actor Daniel Radcliffe (*Harry Potter*) actually appeared in a movie before Harry Potter that few people remember. It was an American film called *The Tailor of Panama,* (2001) and starred Jamie Lee Curtis.

0762.
Actor Jake Gyllenhaal (*October Sky, The Day After Tomorrow*) was offered a role in *The Mighty Ducks*, but his parents didn't want him to go away for two months to shoot it.

0763.
Most people think that George Washington wore a wig, but that was his real hair. He powdered it to make it white, a common practice at the time.

0764.
Rapper Vanilla Ice (*Ice Ice Baby*) has a pet wallaroo named Bucky and a pet goat named Pancho.

0765.
Actor and producer Johnny Depp (*Edward Scissorhands, Pirates of the Caribbean*) knows how to play the guitar.

0766.

Beauty Eva Longoria may be best known as basketball star Tony Parker's ex-wife, but she's an actress too. She starred in *The Young and the Restless* and *Desperate Housewives,* as well as a couple of movies.

0767.

Sharon Osbourne (*The Osbournes, America's Got Talent, The Talk*) wasn't close to her mother. When informed of her mother's death over the phone, she replied, "Oh, what a shame," and put the phone down.

0768.

Actor and wrestler Dwayne Douglas Johnson, known professionally as *The Rock,* wrestled in the WWF under the name Rocky Maivia.

0769.

Actor Bruno Kirby (*City Slickers, When Harry Met Sally, The Godfather Part II*) was born Bruno Giovanni Quidaciolu, Jr. We understand why he changed it.

0770.

Alfred Hitchcock fans remember the caricature of Hitchcock's profile in the opening of *Alfred Hitchcock Presents.* But few know that he drew the caricature himself.

0771.
Miley Ray Cyrus isn't her birth name. She was born Destiny Hope Cyrus on November 23, 1992. We like the original name better.

0772.
Actress Amy Adams (*Man of Steel, American Hustle*) is multi-talented. She also sings, dances, and once entertained thoughts of becoming a professional ballerina.

0773.
Singer, songwriter and actor Usher's first television appearance was on Ed McMahon's *Star Search*, at the tender age of thirteen.

0774.
Former game show host Bob Barker (*Truth of Consequences, The Price is Right*) attended Drury College in Springfield, Missouri on a basketball scholarship.

0775.
Actor Tim Robbins (*Bull Durham, Shawshank Redemption, Mystic River*) played on the same college softball team as another actor, John Cusack.

0776.
Comedian and actor Bob Hope was a four handicap golfer and played until his last years. He died in 2003 at age 100.

0777.
Actress Michelle Rodriguez (*Girlfight, Fast and Furious*) was raised a Jehovah's Witness. She can knock on our door anytime.

0778.
Actor Paul Walker (*Into the Blue, Joy Ride, Fast and Furious*) held a brown belt in Brazilian jiu-jitsu.

0779.
Actress and comedian Lucille Ball's father died when she was only three.

0780.
Singer and actor Clay Aikin (*American Idol*) was once a substitute teacher for special needs children.

0781.
Character actor Fred Gwynne (*The Munsters, My Cousin Vinny*) was best known as his role of Herman, a Frankenstein-like character in *The Munsters*. For that role he had to wear heavy makeup, fifty pounds of padding, and four-inch heels.

0782.
Actress Phoebe Cates (*Fast Times at Ridgemont High, Gremlins*) once received a scholarship to the *School of American Ballet* and went to *Julliard*.

0783.
Actor Bill Murray (*Meatballs, Ghostbusters, Groundhog Day*) was once the lead singer of a rock band called *The Dutch Masters.*

0784.
Actor Bob Crane was most famous for playing Colonel Robert Hogan on *Hogan's Heroes.* But before that, he was a disk jockey.

0785.
Canadian pop star Avril Lavigne (*Complicated, SK8R Boy*), has the name "Brody" tattooed beneath her right breast. Brody was the name of her boyfriend at the time, Brody Jenner. Brody's gone from her life now, but the tattoo's still there.

0786.
Controversial baseball slugger Barry Bonds (*Pittsburgh Pirates, San Francisco Giants*) is the only professional baseball player in history who has hit at least 500 home runs and stolen at least 500 bases.

0787.
Actress Jessica Chastain (*The Help, Zero Dark Thirty*) can thank actor and comedian Robin Williams for her college education. He set up the program that paid for her scholarship.

0788.
Ben Franklin, one of our founding fathers, played the violin, the harp and the guitar. He also invented a vastly improved harmonica.

0789.
Most people just assume that singer and songwriter Dave Matthews (*The Dave Matthews Band*) is from the United States because, well, because he's so talented. When told he wasn't born in the United States they assume he's Canadian because, hey, that's the next best thing, right? Actually, Dave Matthews was born in Johannesburg, South Africa.

0790.
Actress Eliza Dushku (*Buffy the Vampire Slayer, Doll House, Bring it On*) is a vegan.

0791.
Legendary musician Bruce Springsteen wasn't the best student in high school. His former teachers have been quoted as calling him a "loner," and saying all he wanted to do was sit around and play his guitar.

0792.
Singer and actress Jennifer Hudson (*American Idol, Dreamgirls*) took a hiatus from singing temporarily in 2009 after her mother, brother and nephew were murdered.

0793.
Singer and songwriter Bob Dylan is a legend in music. He's also an accomplished artist, and has published several books of his drawings and paintings.

0794.
Former NFL player "Hollywood" Henderson (*Dallas Cowboys*) said Steeler quarterback Terry Bradshaw "couldn't spell the word 'cat' if you spotted him the c and the a." But Bradshaw is no dummy. He's written five books.

0795.
Actress and comedian Lucille Ball suffered from ornithophobia, or a fear of flying birds.

0796.
Lady Gaga was playing the piano at the age of four, and was making public performances at age fourteen.

0797.
David Hasselhoff (*Baywatch, Knight Rider*) is also a fairly successful singer, but he's way more popular in Europe. In 1989 his single *Looking for Freedom* made it number one on German pop charts.

0798.
Famous college and professional football coach Bill Parcels was drafted by the Detroit Lions, but was released before ever playing a single down in the NFL.

0799.
Actor, producer and rapper Will Smith once performed as a rapper named *The Fresh Prince*. The name was derived from his role in *The Fresh Prince of Bel-Air*.

0800.
Singer and actor Clay Aikin (*American Idol*) has a bachelor's degree in special education.

0801.
Character actor Fred Gwynne (*The Munsters, My Cousin Vinny*) was best known as his role of Herman, a Frankenstein-like character in *The Munsters*. In addition to acting, he sang professionally.

0802.
Country music singer Tim McGraw's given name is Sam.

0803.
Actor, model and former rapper Mark Wahlberg (AKA Marky Mark) is a very religious man. A Catholic, he says he attends church daily.

0804.
R&B singer and actress Alicia Keys appeared in an episode of *The Cosby Show* at age four. She was an invited guest at Rudy Huxtable's slumber party.

0805.
Actor and director Jack Nicholson (*One Flew Over the Coocoo's Nest, As Good As It Gets*) could have taken a different path. He was offered a job as a cartoonist, but said he wanted to act instead.

0806.
Actress and producer Kristen Bell (*Veronica Mars, When in Rome*) has a condition called strabismus (lazy eye) in her right eye. She calls that eye "Wonky."

0807.
Harrison Ford (*Star Wars, Indiana Jones*) can fly both airplanes and helicopters.

0808.
Venerable actor Morgan Freeman (*Driving Miss Daisy, Shawshank Redemption, Bruce Almighty*) earned a private pilot's license when he was sixty five years old.

0809.
Elvis Presley received his first guitar for his eleventh birthday. He said he was hoping for a bicycle instead.

0810.
Actor Alec Baldwin (*Hunt for Red October, The Aviator, 30 Rock*) has authored a book, titled *A Promise to Ourselves: A Journey Through Fatherhood and Divorce.*

0811.

Former *Chicago Cubs* and *Atlanta Braves* player Matt Franco is the nephew of actor Kurt Russell (*Swing Shift, Overboard*).

0812.

Actress Farrah Fawcett was born on Ground Hog's Day, February 2, 1947. We wonder if she saw her shadow…

0813.

Actor Paul Newman (*Cool Hand Luke, The Color of Money*) once described himself as a Jew, "because it's more of a challenge."

0814.

In the off season during World War I, baseball player Babe Ruth took a temporary job as a steel mill worker in Pennsylvania, to avoid being drafted for military service.

0815.

Actress and comedian Lucille Ball was once a successful fashion model.

0816.

Actor and producer Ashton Kutcher (*That '70s Show, Two and a Half Men*) used to be a professional model.

0817.
Arnold Schwarzenegger (actor, bodybuilder, governor) was also a pretty good businessman. He was a millionaire at age thirty, before his movie career even started.

0818.
Comedian and actress Ellen DeGeneres (*Mr. Wrong, Finding Nemo, The Ellen DeGeneres Show*) is a distant cousin of Catherine, Duchess of Cambridge.

0819.
Rapper Ja Rule was born in 1976, but has only had nine birthdays. How is that possible, you ask? Because he was born on February 29.

0820.
Actress and director Goldie Hawn (*Laugh-In, Private Benjamin, Best Friends*) is also a talented dancer, trained in ballet and tap.

0821.
Actor and musician Ozzy Osbourne has said he deliberately married his wife Sharon on Independence Day, so he'd never forget his anniversary.

0822.
Singer and actor Clay Aikin (*American Idol*) suffers from TMJ, a genetic jaw disorder.

0823.
Radio personality Howard Stern says what's on his mind. So much so that stations carrying his broadcasts have been fined by the FCC a total of $2.4 million between 1990 and 2004.

0824.
Actress Michelle Rodriguez (*Girlfight, Fast and Furious*) beat out 350 other applicants to win the role as Diana Guzman in *Girlfight*.

0825.
Actress Demi Moore (*St. Elmo's Fire, Indecent Proposal*) once posed for a series of nude photos for *Oui* magazine. Although it's unclear exactly when the photos were taken, Moore has stated she was only sixteen at the time.

0826.
Actress and comedian Lucille Ball once worked as a dancer on Broadway chorus lines, under the alias Diane Belmont.

0827.
Actress Jamie Lee Curtis (*Halloween, True Lies*) was born to be in horror movies. After all, her mother was Janet Leigh, who took the most remembered shower in film history, in *Psycho*.

0828.
Actor Woody Harrelson (*Cheers, White Men Can't Jump*) is a "truther," who believes that the 911 attacks were carried out with the help of the U.S. government.

0829.
Dallas Cowboys football coach Tom Landry has been gone for awhile now, having died in 2000. But he still holds several distinctive records. One of them is the number of consecutive winning seasons, with twenty.

0830.
George Washington was quite the dancer, and always had the ladies lined up at formal balls and parties.

0831.
Before she hit it big, singer Kelly Clarkson (*American Idol*) once worked at a comedy club as a cocktail waitress.

0832.
One of actor Robert Deniro's most memorable roles was as a young Vito Corleone in *The Godfather Part II.* If he'd had his way, though, he would have been in the original. He tried out for the role of Michael Corleone in the original *Godfather,* but lost out to Al Pacino.

0833.
Actor Jake Gyllenhaal (*October Sky, The Day After Tomorrow*) auditioned as Spider-Man in *Spider-Man 2* and as Batman in *Batman Begins* but didn't get either role.

0834.
Rapper Vanilla Ice (*Ice Ice Baby*) also knows how to play the drums, bass and keyboard.

0835.
Race car driver Danika Patrick was a cheerleader in high school.

0836.
Former game show host Bob Barker (*Truth of Consequences, The Price is Right*) was a fighter pilot in the U.S. Navy during World War II.

0837.
Author Darrell Maloney (*The Cleansing, The Legend of Mary and Bill*) almost drowned when he was twelve. A mysterious figure pulled him from murky lake waters and then seemingly disappeared. To this day Maloney believes he was rescued by his dead grandfather.

0838.
Beauty Eva Longoria (*Young and the Restless, Desperate Housewives*) once worked behind the counter at a Wendy's Restaurant.

0839.
Sharon Osbourne (*The Osbournes, America's Got Talent, The Talk*) was often the victim of violence from her husband Ozzy. He once knocked out her front teeth.

0840.
Actor and producer Johnny Depp (*Edward Scissorhands, Pirates of the Caribbean*) once worked as a telemarketer.

0841.
Comedian and actor Bob Hope didn't die until 2003. But that didn't stop the U.S. House of Representatives from mistakenly announcing his death in 1998.

0842.
Actor Bruno Kirby (*City Slickers, When Harry Met Sally, The Godfather Part II*) also appeared in the pilot episode of *M*A*S*H**, in a non-speaking role.

0843.
Singer and actress Miley Cyrus has an "equals" tattoo on her right ring finger, to symbolize her support for gay and lesbian equality.

0844.
When actress Amy Adams (*Man of Steel, American Hustle*) graduated from high school at the age of eighteen, she took her first full time job at *Hooters.*

0845.
Singer, songwriter and actor Usher is part owner of the Cleveland Cavaliers basketball team.

0846.
Actor and wrestler Dwayne Douglas Johnson, known professionally as *The Rock,* is a descendent of Samoan Chiefs on his mother's side.

0847.
Actor Vin Diesel (*Saving Private Ryan, Fast and Furious*) has never met his biological father.

0848.
Actress Jordana Brewster (*The Faculty, Fast and Furious*) may have that American girl next door look. But actually she is Brazilian-American.

0849.
Actress and comedian Lucille Ball wasn't really a redhead. She was a brunette.

0850.
Singer and songwriter Bob Marley died at age 36.

0851.
Character actor Fred Gwynne (*The Munsters, My Cousin Vinny*) was best known as his role of Herman, a Frankenstein-like character in *The Munsters*. He was also an accomplished painter.

0852.
Actress Phoebe Cates (*Fast Times at Ridgemont High, Gremlins*) was once a professional model, but quit because it was too monotonous. She said, "It's just the same thing, over and over…"

0853.
Founding father Benjamin Franklin spoke fluent Italian.

0854.
Actor Tim Robbins (*Bull Durham, Shawshank Redemption, Mystic River*) is the tallest winner of an Academy Award, at 6'5".

0855.
Charles Elwood "Chuck" Yeager was the man who broke the sound barrier in 1947. He was one of the most experienced test pilots the United States Air Force had when the space program cranked up, and the most logical person to be one of the first astronauts. But NASA shunned him because despite all his experience and accomplishments, he didn't fit their image. Because he never went to college.

0856.
Actor Bill Murray (*Meatballs, Ghostbusters, Groundhog Day*) was once arrested in Chicago for possession with intent to sell ten pounds of marijuana. He was sentenced to probation.

0857.
Actor Bob Crane was most famous for playing Colonel Robert Hogan on *Hogan's Heroes*. In 1978, he was found murdered, beaten to death in Scottsdale, Arizona. The murder remains unsolved.

0858.
Pop star Michael Jackson was (and still is) one of the most recognizable figures in the world. But do you know his middle name? It's Joseph.

0859.
Actress Jessica Chastain (*The Help, Zero Dark Thirty*) has a three-legged dog named Chaplin.

0860.
Actor Bill Murray (*Meatballs, Ghostbusters, Groundhog Day*) is very much anti-Hollywood. He has no agent or manager and only checks his voicemail occasionally.

0861.
Actor, comedian and singer Dean Martin was born Dino Paul Crocetti. He spoke only Italian until he started grade school and they taught him English.

0862.
Actress and comedian Lucille Ball was a registered member of the Communist Party.

0863.
Actor Chevy Chase (*Saturday Night Live, National Lampoon*) was once expelled from a private school for having a cow in his dorm room.

0864.
Legendary musician Bruce Springsteen wasn't a fan of high school. In fact, he skipped his own graduation ceremony.

0865.
NFL legend Warren Sapp is best known, of course, as a powerful defensive tackle. But he had other skills as well. He still holds the Apopka (Florida) High School record for longest field goal.

0866.
Singer and songwriter Bob Dylan was born Robert Allen Zimmerman. We already mentioned that previously. But he was also given a Hebrew name. It's Shabtai Zisl ben Avraham.

0867.
Steven Spielberg (*Jurassic Park, Lincoln, Schindler's List*) is one of the most revered directors in the history of cinema. He's also dyslexic.

0868.
David Hasselhoff (*Baywatch, Knight Rider*) wasn't an immediate success. *Baywatch* was cancelled after the first season, and only after Hasselhoff bought the rights to it and started producing it himself did it make a comeback.

0869.
Some might say it doesn't fit her character, but Lady Gaga went to an all girl Catholic School. And she was an excellent student.

0870.
Country music singer Tim McGraw has said that in college his roommates kept hiding his guitar because he played so badly.

0871.
Actress Michelle Rodriguez (*Girlfight, Fast and Furious*) is also a very talented screenwriter.

0872.
Singer and songwriter Bob Marley was a committed Rastafarian.

0873.
Actor Bill Murray (*Meatballs, Ghostbusters, Groundhog Day*) once did a parachute jump with the United States Army's elite Golden Knights parachute demonstration team.

0874.
In 2010, venerable actor Morgan Freeman (*Driving Miss Daisy, Shawshank Redemption, Bruce Almighty*) took over voiceover duties for the CBS Evening News. He replaced Walter *"And that's the way it is…"* Cronkite.

0875.
In her divorce filing, actress and comedian Lucille Ball described being married to actor and entertainer Desi Arnaz "a nightmare."

0876.
Famed home run hitter of the New York Yankees Babe Ruth caught the flu in 1925, fainted and was rushed to the hospital. Several British newspapers wrongly reported that he was dead.

0877.
Harrison Ford (*Star Wars, Indiana Jones*), a licensed pilot himself, has flown with the U.S. Navy's Blue Angels flight demonstration team.

0878.
The only actor in history to have eight consecutive films gross over $100 million in the domestic box office: Will Smith.

0879.
Actor, model and former rapper Mark Wahlberg (AKA Marky Mark) has several tattoos, including Tweety Bird, Bob Marley, and rosary beads.

0880.
Sultry R&B singer and actress Alicia Keys is also an accomplished pianist.

0881.
Actor and director Jack Nicholson (*One Flew Over the Coocoo's Nest, As Good As It Gets*) was a next door neighbor to Marlon Brando for years. When Brando died, Nicholson bought his estate and had it demolished.

0882.
Actress and producer Kristen Bell (*Veronica Mars, When in Rome*) went by the name Annie until she was a freshman in high school. She didn't like her first name. Anne was her middle name.

0883.
Actor, comedian and singer Dean Martin could play the drums.

0884.
Elvis Presley's eighth grade music teacher told him he had no aptitude for singing.

0885.
Actor Alec Baldwin (*Hunt for red October, The Aviator, 30 Rock*) confided to *Playboy* magazine that he contemplated suicide in 2007.

0886.
Actor and producer Ashton Kutcher (*That '70s Show, Two and a Half Men*) has a twin brother.

0887.
Actor Paul Newman (*Cool Hand Luke, The Color of Money*) was a veteran, having served in the United States Navy during World War II.

0888.
In 1947 Chuck Yeager was flying experimental aircraft and became the first man to break the sound barrier at Edwards Air Force Base in southern California. But he'd come a very long way. A mere six years before, he was just another lowly Air Force enlisted mechanic, fixing airplanes at George Air Force Base, a few miles away at Victorville.

0889.
Actress Farrah Fawcett was named "Ferrah" on her birth certificate. She later changed the spelling to Farrah, which she thought was more suited for a girl.

0890.
Rapper Ja Rule was raised a Jehovah's Witness.

0891.
Singer and songwriter Dave Matthews (*The Dave Matthews Band*) once had a regular job, working for IBM.

0892.
Actor and dancer Patrick Swayze (*Dirty Dancing, Ghost*) was also a singer and songwriter.

0893.
Comedian and actress Ellen DeGeneres (*Mr. Wrong, Finding Nemo, The Ellen DeGeneres Show*) hosted the first Emmy Awards show after the Sept 11, 2001 attacks. She opened with the line "What would bug the Taliban more than seeing a gay woman in a suit, surrounded by Jews?"

0894.
When actor Robert DeNiro (*Goodfellas, The Godfather Part II*) was a boy, he had a rather pale complexion. His childhood friends in Manhattan's Little Italy neighborhood nicknamed him "Bobby Milk."

0895.
Actress and director Goldie Hawn (*Laugh-In, Private Benjamin, Best Friends*) also sings, and recorded a Country album for Warner Brothers Records called *Goldie*.

0896.
Arnold Schwarzenegger (actor, bodybuilder, governor) bought the very first Hummer ever made for civilian use.

0897.
Actor and musician Ozzy Osbourne's first tattoos were the letters O,Z,Z and Y across his left knuckles. He did the tattoos himself, with a sewing needle and pencil lead.

0898.
Actor, comedian and singer Dean Martin was the father-in-law of *Beach Boys* singer Carl Wilson, Olympic figure skater Dorothy Hamill, and actress Olivia Hussey.

0899.
Actor Tom Cruise (*Outsiders, Taps, Mission: Impossible*) was born Thomas Cruise Mopather IV. There were three others before him.

0900.
Actress Jamie Lee Curtis (*Halloween, True Lies*) has another name. In Britain, where she married Baron Christopher Guest, her name is Lady Haden-Guest.

0901.
Actor Jake Gyllenhaal (*October Sky, The Day After Tomorrow*) cooks and builds furniture to relax.

0902.
Contrary to popular belief, George Washington's teeth were not made of wood. They were made from hippopotamus and elephant ivory.

0903.
Race car driver Danika Patrick appears as a character in the video game *Sonic and All-Stars Racing Transformed.*

0904.

Dallas Cowboys football coach Tom Landry didn't like the term "America's Team, a tag sports media put on the Cowboys in the 1970s.

0905.

Former game show host Bob Barker (*Truth of Consequences, The Price is Right*) has been a vegetarian since 1979.

0906.

Singer Ozzy Osbourne was once arrested for attempted murder. The victim: his wife Sharon.

0907.

Beauty Eva Longoria (*Young and the Restless, Desperate Housewives*) won the title of Miss Corpus Christi (Texas) in 1998.

0908.

Actor Ben Affleck (*Pearl Harbor*) has activism in his blood. His mother Christine was a freedom rider in the 1960s.

0909.

On his death bed, comedian and actor Bob Hope's wife asked him where he wanted to be buried. He said, "Surprise me."

0910.
Actress Demi Moore (*St. Elmo's Fire, Indecent Proposal*) was married to musician Freddy Moore, who at that time was lead singer of the group *Boy*. While they were married, she co-wrote several songs with him.

0911.
Actor Dan Akroyd was a reserve commander for the Harahan, Louisiana Police Department.

0912.
Actor Bruno Kirby (*City Slickers, When Harry Met Sally, The Godfather Part II*) was very allergic to horses. He had to get a daily shot on set while filming *City Slickers*.

0913.
Actor Vin Diesel (*Saving Private Ryan, Fast and Furious*) changed his name from Mark Sinclair to Vin Diesel while working as a night club bouncer.

0914.
Actress Jordana Brewster (*The Faculty, Fast and Furious*) got her start in soap operas. She worked on *All My Children* and *As The World Turns.*

0915.
Actress and comedian Lucille Ball used to pick up radio signals in the fillings of her teeth.

0916.
Actor, comedian and singer Dean Martin was once a boxer who fought under the name "Kid Crochet."

0917.
Actress Jordana Brewster (*The Faculty, Fast and Furious*) is of Brazilian and American heritage. But she was born in Panama City, Panama.

0918.
Actor Woody Harrelson (*Cheers, White Men Can't Jump*) is neither a Republican nor a Democrat. He describes himself as an "anarchist."

0919.
Cornelius Crane Chase, better known as Chevy Chase (*Saturday Night Live, National Lampoon*) is descended from the Kanienkehaka Indian tribe, better known as the Mohawks.

0920.
Actor, comedian and singer Dean Martin died on Christmas Day, in 1995.

0921.
Actress Phoebe Cates (*Fast Times at Ridgemont High, Gremlins*) is a talented singer as well. She sang two songs on the soundtrack of one of her movies, *Private School*.

0922.
Mention the name Johnny Unitas to any football fan and they'll conjure up a vision of the striking quarterback in a Baltimore Colt uniform. A lot of people have forgotten that he also played for the Pittsburgh Steelers and San Diego Chargers.

0923.
Character actor Fred Gwynne (*The Munsters, My Cousin Vinny*) was best known as his role of Herman, a Frankenstein-like character in *The Munsters.* He was also a very talented artist who illustrated children's books.

0924.
Singer and songwriter Bob Marley's cancer started in his toe. Doctors wanted to amputate it but he refused on religious grounds. The cancer soon spread to the rest of his body and killed him.

0925.
Actor Joe Pesci (*Goodfellas, Casino, My Cousin Vinny*) was once a barber.

0926.
Actor, comedian and singer Dean Martin was once a soldier. He was drafted into the United States Army during World War II, but was discharged after only a year.

0927.
Ben Franklin was an avid chess player, and was believed to be the first chess player in North America. He was later inducted into the U.S. Chess Hall of Fame.

0928.
Actor Tim Robbins (*Bull Durham, Shawshank Redemption, Mystic River*) is an avid hockey fan, and plays hockey in a New York City recreational league.

0929.
Actress Michelle Rodriguez (*Girlfight, Fast and Furious*) has a second job. She has been a professional disc jockey since 2009.

0930.
Remember that "Melkor" tattoo actor Vin Diesel (*Saving Private Ryan, Fast and Furious*) had on his stomach in the 30th anniversary edition of *Dragon* magazine? It was fake.

0931.
Radio personality Howard Stern is a talented chess player who has achieved a rating of over 1600.

0932.
Actor Tommy Lee Jones (*Lonesome Dove, Men in Black*) is part Cherokee Indian.

0933.
Actor Johnny Galecki (*Rosanne, The Big Bang Theory*) was born in Belgium. His father was in the United States Air Force and the family was stationed there.

0934.
Director and producer Alfred Hitchcock is regarded as one of the best producers of horror films, even thirty years after his death. He was British by birth, and didn't even become an American citizen until 1955.

0935.
Actress Demi Moore (*St. Elmo's Fire, Indecent Proposal*) is an avid doll collector. At one time, she maintained a separate residence just for her 2,000 dolls.

0936.
Pop star Michael Jackson was (and still is) one of the most recognizable figures in the world. Everybody remembers the Jackson five, but there were more Jacksons. Michael was the eighth of ten children.

0937.
Actor Bob Crane was most famous for playing Colonel Robert Hogan on *Hogan's Heroes*. But he was also passionate about music. He was a good drummer and a passable bugler.

0938.
Pop star singer, songwriter and actress Christina Aguilera was a military brat. Her father was in the United States Army and she lived in several places throughout the United States. As well as Japan.

0939.
Famed home run hitter of the New York Yankees Babe Ruth actually finished his career with the Boston Braves.

0940.
Country music singer Tim McGraw was generally well reviewed for his role as an overbearing father in 2004's *Friday Night Lights.*

0941.
Comedian and actor Bob Hope's Palm Springs home was built to resemble a volcano. It was sold in 2013 for "around $50 million."

0942.
Tonight Show host Jay Leno could have had surgery to reset his mandible and lessen his prominent chin, but he's never done it because he doesn't want his mouth wired shut for an extended time.

0943.
Sharon Osbourne (*The Osbournes, America's Got Talent, The Talk*) lost a hundred pounds after having lap band surgery in 1999.

0944.
Former Pittsburgh Steeler quarterback Terry Bradshaw has recorded six country music albums. His rendition of *I'm So Lonesome I Could Cry* made the *Billboard* Top 20.

0945.
Legendary musician Bruce Springsteen was a college drop-out. But that's okay. He seems to have done quite well despite that.

0946.
When he was in high school, Bob Dylan and his band once played a rock and roll concert that upset the principal so much he turned off the microphones.

0947.
David Hasselhoff (*Baywatch, Knight Rider*) played a pay-per-view concert in Atlantic City to launch his American singing career. But the concert wasn't as successful as was expected. Most of America was busy watching O.J. Simpson's low speed chase in a white Bronco that same day.

0948.
Lady Gaga says she's nothing like her on-stage persona. She describes herself as "a real family girl... very old-fashioned...and quite down to earth."

0949.
Beauty Eva Longoria (*Young and the Restless, Desperate Housewives*) is half owner of a restaurant called "Beso" (Kiss) in Hollywood.

0950.
George Washington owned slaves.

0951.
Actress Katie Holmes (*Dawson's Creek, Abandon*) was a straight-A student in high school.

0952.
Actor, producer and rapper Will Smith once attended three premiers in twenty four hours. He won a place in the *Guinness Book of World Records* for that.

0953.
Rapper and actor Eminem (born Marshall Bruce Mathers III) took a long time to join the world. His mother was in labor for 73 hours, and it is said she almost died during the delivery.

0954.
Harrison Ford (*Star Wars, Indiana Jones*) has a spider named after him: the *Calponia harrisonfordi*. Seriously.

0955.
Actress Kate Winslet (*The Titanic, Sense and Sensibility*) has a set of pipes too. She's even been awarded a Grammy to prove it.

0956.
Venerable actor Morgan Freeman (*Driving Miss Daisy, Shawshank Redemption, Bruce Almighty*) had a bad automobile accident in 2008. For a long time, he lost use of the fingers on his left hand.

0957.
Actress and producer Kristen Bell (*Veronica Mars, When in Rome*) once played in a theater production of *Raggedy Ann and Andy*. Actually, she played two roles: a tree and a banana.

0958.
Actor and director Jack Nicholson (*One Flew Over the Coocoo's Nest, As Good As It Gets*) has held season courtside seats at Los Angels Lakers games for the past twenty five years.

0959.
Recently retired and future Hall of Famer Chipper Jones of the *Atlanta Braves* got his nickname from his father, who thought he was a "chip off the old block." His given name is Larry.

0960.
Chuck Yeager, the first man to fly faster than the speed of sound, was an excellent hunter. He once shot a deer at six hundred yards. That's almost half a mile away.

0961.
Elvis Presley was often bullied in high school, where he was called a "sissy" and a "mama's boy."

0962.
Actress Farrah Fawcett (*Charlie's Angels, The Burning Bed*) was voted "most beautiful" by her classmates all four years she was in high school.

0963.
Actor and dancer Patrick Swayze (*Dirty Dancing, Ghost*) was a distant cousin of famous newsman John Cameron Swayze.

0964.
Actor Paul Newman (*Cool Hand Luke, The Color of Money*) was on his way to battle aboard the USS Bunker Hill during World War II, but was delayed because his pilot had an ear infection. The rest of the detail that went on without him were all killed in the battle.

0965.
George Washington's father died when George was eleven, and he was raised by an older half-brother.

0966.
Actress and director Goldie Hawn (*Laugh-In, Private Benjamin, Best Friends*) was once married to Gus Trikonis, who played a shark in *West Side Story.*

0967.
Actor Robert DeNiro was the first actor to win an Academy Award speaking mainly a foreign language for his role in *The Godfather Part II.* In the movie, he spoke mainly in Sicilian, with English subtitles.

0968.
Actor and producer Ashton Kutcher (*That '70s Show, Two and a Half Men*) once revealed that he contemplated suicide at age 13, so that his ill brother could have his heart.

0969.
Former game show host Bob Barker (*The Bob Barker Show, Truth or Consequences, The Price is Right*) holds the record for holding down a weekday daytime hosting job. Between his three shows, he served in that role for 51 years.

0970.
Race car driver Danika Patrick made an appearance on the TV show *CSI:NY.* She played a race car driver suspected of murder.

0971.
The first United States Postmaster General was Benjamin Franklin.

0972.
Actress Jamie Lee Curtis (*Halloween, True Lies*) has written and published ten children's books.

0973.
Actor and director Alan Alda (*M*A*S*H*, The West Wing*) was best known for his role as Hawkeye Pierce. He actually was in the Army, and was stationed at Ft. Benning, Georgia.

0974.
Actor Tom Cruise (*Outsiders, Taps, Mission: Impossible*) played linebacker on his high school football team, until he was kicked off the team. He was caught drinking a beer before a game.

0975.
Singer-songwriter and actor Justin Timberlake (*'N Sync, Friends With Benefits*) made his first TV appearance on Ed McMahon's *Star Search* under the name Justin Randall. He was eleven at the time.

0976.
Actor and musician Ozzy Osbourne once urinated on a cenotaph in front of the Alamo, while wearing a dress. He was banned from San Antonio for ten years.

0977.
Country music sweetheart Miranda Lambert is an avid deer hunter.

0978.

Singer-songwriter and actor Justin Timberlake (*'N Sync, Friends With Benefits*) has OCD *and* ADHD.

0979.

Nicolas Kim Coppola wanted to be an actor, but he didn't want people to say he only got roles because he was the nephew of famed director Francis Ford Coppola. So he changed his name to Nicolas Cage. He got the name from a comic book character.

0980.

If actor Matt Damon and actor Ben Affleck seem comfortable on screen together, it might be because they go back a long way. They were childhood friends who lived two blocks apart.

0981.

Actress Farrah Fawcett (*Charlie's Angels, The Burning Bed*) is equally well known for a poster she made in a red bathing suit. When she posed for that famous photo, she styled her own hair and did her own makeup. Without a mirror.

0982.

Actor and dancer Patrick Swayze (*Dirty Dancing, Ghost*) played football in high school and was hoping to play professionally someday, until a knee injury ended his career.

0983.
Actor Paul Newman (*Cool Hand Luke, The Color of Money*) was married to actress Joanne Woodward for fifty years.

0984.
The only class Elvis Presley ever failed in high school was music.

0985.
Actor Tim Robbins (*Bull Durham, Shawshank Redemption, Mystic River*) has had some great roles for sure. But who remembers he also played in a movie called *Howard the Duck*? He was nominated for a *Razzie Award* for worst actor.

0986.
Venerable actor Morgan Freeman (*Driving Miss Daisy, Shawshank Redemption, Bruce Almighty*) doesn't support the celebration of Black History Month. He says the only way to end racism is to stop talking about it.

0987.
Actress Kate Winslet (*The Titanic, Sense and Sensibility*) sang the soundtrack of *Heavenly Creatures* (1992).

0988.
Actor and producer Leonardo DiCaprio (*The Aviator, What's eating Gilbert Grape, Titanic*) is named Leonardo because his mother was looking at a Leonardo DaVinci painting the first time he kicked.

0989.

Actress and producer Kristen Bell (*Veronica Mars, When in Rome*) owns a black lab named Sadie. Sadie was rescued from New Orleans after Hurricane Katrina and adopted by Bell.

0990.

Actor and director Jack Nicholson (*One Flew Over the Coocoo's Nest, As Good As It Gets*) is an avid art collector. His extensive collection includes works by Matisse, Warhol and Vettriano.

0991.

Eminem has been very successful in both rapping and acting. But that wasn't his first career choice. He aspired to become a comic book illustrator before discovering his musical talents.

0992.

Lady Gaga's aunt Joanne Germanotta died twelve years before Gaga's birth. But the singer feels such an attachment to her deceased aunt that she tattooed her death date "somewhere on her body."

0993.

In 2002, Johnny Unitas Stadium was dedicated in Towson, Maryland. Unitas was there for the event, and threw his very last pass for the cameras. He died five days later.

0994.
Bob Dylan loves poetry. So much so, that when he created his stage name, he chose Dylan after poet Dylan Thomas.

0995.
Walt Disney was a staunch anti-communist. When U.S Senator Joe McCarthy held hearings before the House Un-American Activities Committee, Disney appeared and testified. He accused several labor union organizers of being communists.

0996.
Legendary musician Bruce Springsteen was inspired to take up music after he saw Elvis Presley perform on *The Ed Sullivan Show*. Bruce was seven at the time.

0997.
If you've ever seen the movie classic *The Right Stuff,* you'll remember the memorable performance of Sam Shepard, who played the part of Chuck Yeager. But did you know that the real Chuck Yeager- the man who broke the sound barrier- was also in the film? The real Mr. Yeager played Fred, the old codger who hung around Pancho's bar in several of the scenes throughout the movie.

0998.
Recently retired and future Hall of Famer Chipper Jones of the *Atlanta Braves* is an avid deer hunter. He was co-owner of a hunting show called *Buck Commander*, which introduced Willie Robertson (*Duck Dynasty*) to the world.

0999.
Dallas Cowboys football coach Tom Landry wasn't just a great coach. He was a great quarterback too. In his high school days, he led Mission High School (Texas) to an undefeated season.

1000.
Actor Tommy Lee Jones (*Lonesome Dove, Men in Black*), is a smart dude. He attended Harvard University. As a freshman, his dorm room was across the hall from future Vice President Al Gore.

1001.
Dave Matthews is best known for his singing and songwriting talents, and as the front man for *The Dave Matthews Band*. But he's also tried his hand at acting, including not very memorable roles in *Because of Winn Dixie* and *I Now Pronounce You Chuck and Larry*.

REFERENCES

Gary McGee: *Band on the Run*

Biography.com: *Marilyn Monroe*

The Daily Telegraph: *The Child Who Became a Star: Madonna*

Philip Norman: *John Lennon, The Life*

Internet Movie Database

Country Weekly: *Bubbly Beauty*

George Rose: *The Man in Black*

Graham Calkin: *Anthology* (2008)

William Ruhlman: *Beginnings*

Why Buddy Holly Still Matters Today: *The Independent*

Famous Masons: *MWGLNY*

Trivia: Sonny and Cher: *Weekly World News*

Rolling Stone Magazine: *Taylor Swift Revealed*

wfmu.org: *The Early David Letterman*

Pocket Books: *The Star Trek Encyclopedia*

William Shatner: *Star Trek Memories*

The Family Dynamic: *EW Weekly*

Doo-Wops and Hooligans: Amazon.com

"Science Fiction," *Pioneers of Television, PBS*

The Sydney Morning Herald: *Trial by Fury, 2004*

Marquis: *Who's Who in America*

Filmreference.com: *Andy Griffith Biography*

Island Net: *Chronology of the Walt Disney Company*

Wikipedia.com

E. Whittaker: *Albert Einstein, 1879-1955*

Sarah Palin: *Going Rogue* (2009)

Noah Dietrich and Bob Thomas: *Howard: The Amazing Mr. Hughes*

Brad Pitt on Another World: *The Another World Home Page*

The Celebrity 100: Forbes Magazine

The Fifty Greatest TV Icons: James Gandolfini. (Entertainment Weekly)

Gerald Clarke, *Get Happy: The Life of Judy Garland*

*****

I hope you've enjoyed reading
1001 Little Known Things About Well Known
People.
Please watch out for the sequel,
1002 Things You Didn't Know About Celebrities,
Coming in the fall of 2014.

*****

In the meantime, please enjoy this preview of
1001 Funny and Witty Twitter Tweets,
By Charlie Bennett.
Available now on Amazon.com and through
Barnes and Noble Booksellers.

*****

0001.
You can't buy happiness, but you can buy ice cream.
And that's kind of the same thing.

0002.
If Plan A fails, remember that you have twenty five
letters left.

0003.
Take your mom to dinner tonight. It's only fair, since you're the reason she drinks.

0004.
Things to do today: (1) Get up. (2) Be awesome. (3) Go back to bed.

0005.
You might be a redneck if you come back from the dump with more than you took.

0006.
Wouldn't it be nice if the world was flat? Then we could just push off the people we didn't like.

0007.
Sarcasm is a better option than beating the hell out of people.

0008.
Women say they love men in uniform, but when I wear my work clothes from McDonald's they won't even talk to me.

0009.
I finally found out what women really want. Security. At least that's what they yell when I try to talk to them.

0010.
Always pay the bill from your exorcist. Otherwise you'll be repossessed.

0011.
The most important thing in life is to be yourself. Unless you can be Batman. If you can be Batman, then forget what I said and be Batman.

0012.
I'm not really paranoid, but I know that all of you think I am.

0013.
I was good at math until they decided to mix the alphabet in it.

0014.
You never know what you have until you clean your house.

0015.
The reason I'm me is because Superman was already taken. I'm the next best thing.

0016.
The best way to make someone remember you is to loan them money.

0017.
The reason I'm sarcastic is because shooting people in the head is frowned upon.

0018.
There are three kinds of people in this world: those who are good at math, and those who aren't.

0019.
My dog winks at me sometimes. I always wink back, in case it's some kind of code.

0020.
Nothing ruins a good Friday like realizing it's only Tuesday.

0021.

I've learned that pleasing everyone is impossible. But pissing everybody off is a piece of cake.

0022.

Say what you mean. Mean what you say. But don't say it mean.

0023.

I love gossip. I always find out things about myself I never knew before.

0024.

When I die, I want the coroner to write down my cause of death as: "He laid down the boogie and played that funky music 'til he died."

0025.

I'm not always right, but when I am it's usually all of the time.

0026.

Lazy rule number 6: If it's not on the first page of a Google search, it doesn't exist.

0027.
I just saved a ton of money on car insurance by backing up and leaving the scene of the accident.

0028.
I just saved a ton of money on Christmas gifts by discussing politics on Facebook.

0029.
Be careful what you say to old people. They don't like being old in the first place, so it doesn't make much to piss them off.

0030.
If time is money, are ATMs time machines?

0031.
The word "phonetically" doesn't even start with an f. Stuff like that is why aliens fly right past us.

0032.
Life is like chocolate candy. Occasionally you're just gonna have to deal with a few nuts.

0033.
Every day, millions of fruits and vegetables are needlessly slaughtered by vegetarians. When is the violence going to end?

0034.
Never argue with stupid people. They will drag you down to their level and beat you with experience.

0035.
I don't want to brag or anything, but I do more dumb things before 9 a.m. than most people do all day.

0036.
My dog thinks I'm awesome. He also thinks eating poop and sniffing butts is awesome. But mostly me.

0037.
Life is short. Smile while you still have teeth.

0038.
Here's a depressing thought. Just think of how stupid the average person is. Then consider that half of them are stupider than that.

0039.
Please don't throw your cigarette butts in the urinals. It makes them soggy and hard to light.

0040.
Any day I make it to sundown without shooting anyone is a good day.

0041.
I just found a whip, a mask and handcuffs in my mom's bedroom. I can't believe it. My mom's a superhero!

0042.
I'm not totally useless. I can be used as a bad example.

0043.
Becoming a vegetarian is a huge missed steak.

0044.
Okay, if we get caught and arrested, here's the story…

0045.

It's so cold outside today, I actually saw a gangsta pull his pants up.

0046.

If you think that your dog can't count, try letting him see you put three dog biscuits into your pocket, and then only giving him two of them.

0047.

Roses are red, violets are blue. Tequila is cheaper than dinner for two.

0048.

Why haven't they invented a smoke detector that can tell the difference between a burned piece of toast and a raging inferno?

0049.

I'm not saying that you're crazy. I'm just suggesting that you're one buckle short of a straight jacket.

0050.

God gave us friends to make up for our relatives.

0051.
The reason the internet is full of cats is because dog people actually go outside.

0052.
When someone rings the door bell, why do dogs always assume it's for them?

0053.
Don't take life so seriously. It's not like you're going to get out alive.

0054.
It's a free country. Eat whatever you want. If anyone tries to lecture you about your weight, eat them too.

0055.
I'm ready to go. Just remember, if we get caught, I'm deaf and you don't speak English.

0056.
There are a lot of people who should thank their lucky stars that everything I wish for does not come true.

0057.

I don't mind going to work every day. But that eight hour wait to go home every afternoon really sucks.

0058.

I don't like making plans for the day, because then that pesky word "premeditation" starts getting thrown around the courtroom.